PRIVATE
HITLER'S
WAR
1914-1918

BY
BOB CARRUTHERS

Pen & Sword
MILITARY

This edition published in 2014 by

Pen & Sword Military
An imprint of
Pen & Sword Books Ltd
47 Church Street
Barnsley
South Yorkshire
S70 2AS

ISBN: 9781473822764

A CIP catalogue record for this book is available from the British Library

Printed and bound in England
By CPI Group (UK) Ltd, Croydon, CR0 4YY

Pen & Sword Books Ltd incorporates the imprints of Pen & Sword Aviation, Pen & Sword Family History, Pen & Sword Maritime, Pen & Sword Military, Pen & Sword Discovery, Pen & Sword Politics, Pen & Sword Atlas, Pen & Sword Archaeology, Wharncliffe Local History, Wharncliffe True Crime, Wharncliffe Transport, Pen & Sword Select, Pen & Sword Military Classics, Leo Cooper, The Praetorian Press, Claymore Press, Remember When, Seaforth Publishing and Frontline Publishing

For a complete list of Pen & Sword titles please contact
PEN & SWORD BOOKS LIMITED
47 Church Street, Barnsley, South Yorkshire, S70 2AS, England
E-mail: enquiries@pen-and-sword.co.uk
Website: www.pen-and-sword.co.uk

CONTENTS

'THE SOLDIER HAS A BOUNDLESS
AFFECTION FOR THE GROUND ON
WHICH HE HAS SHED HIS BLOOD.'

ADOLF HITLER, AUGUST 1942

INTRODUCTION

FOR THE LAST THIRTY YEARS THROUGH MY work as a film maker and writer I have often found myself immersed in the murky world of Adolf Hitler. He is one of the most public figures of the twentieth century yet much of his life remains in shadow. He had much to hide and certainly did a good job in obscuring the detail of much of his early life. For many years I have been of the opinion that the stimulus of German nationalism, his nihilistic willingness to take risks and an innate love of violence for the sake of violence, were the key factors which shaped Hitler's *weltanschauung* (or world view). I was also fascinated by the influence of the pan-German nationalist agenda on the decisions which shaped his personal life, and among those key decisions was his choice, in 1914, to enlist as a volunteer in the Imperial German Army.

Despite all of the millions of words written a comprehensive picture of the man behind the myth remains as elusive as ever. One source of frustration for me was that I was never able to find a single volume which dealt adequately with Hitler's service in the Great War without wandering off into a survey of the course of the whole war. For me the primary sources of history are the key to every question and I find it endlessly frustrating when a potentially illuminating primary source passage is cut short. Earlier this year I finally found the time to begin work on what I hoped would be a short and succinct work which kept the focus on the subject of Hitler's personal experience in the Great War and allowed the primary sources to speak for themselves. In order to advance the primary source theme I have relied extensively on quotations from Hitler's own version of events as published by him in the pages of *'Mein Kampf'*. In doing so I have relied entirely upon the 1936 translation by James Murphy, as published in the United Kingdom by Hutchinson and Co Ltd. This was the only officially sanctioned version during the Nazi era and as such it seems the most appropriate source for English readers. I am grateful to Pen and Sword, my publishers, who have made possible this edition and to Coda Publishing who make available the entire Murphy text for study and reference.

Hitler began work on his book sometime after November 1923 while imprisoned in the fortress of Landsberg. We know that Hitler received many visitors earlier on, but soon devoted himself entirely to writing 'Mein Kampf', the bulk of which must therefore have been written in 1924. The prison governor of Landsberg noted at the time that 'he (Hitler) hopes the book will run into many editions, thus enabling him to fulfil his financial obligations and to defray the expenses incurred at the time of his trial.' 'Mein Kampf' is routinely dismissed as unreadable and this was certainly the case in contemporary circles where many Nazi functionaries, including Göring, privately joked that they had never read the thing. Italian Fascist dictator and Nazi ally, Benito Mussolini, was famously critical, stating that the book was '... a boring tome that I have never been able to read.' He also remarked that Hitler's beliefs, as expressed in the book, were '... little more than commonplace clichés.' For students of history, politics and general readers with an interest in the Great War period that is certainly not the case. While it is true those large sections of political exposition are rambling and turgid, they do nonetheless repay the reader with an insight into the workings of the mind of Adolf Hitler. However, the book also contains highly accessible elements of autobiography which are intriguing as they afford us the ultimate primary source glimpse into the private world of Adolf Hitler during the Great War. On balance I'm sure most readers would side with Winston Churchill who stated, shortly after Hitler's ascension to power, that no other book deserved more intensive scrutiny. I still believe that Churchill was right and when it comes to the study of Hitler in the Great War 'Mein Kampf' should not be dismissed as readily as is so often the case. However, we should never lose sight of the fact that Hitler was a masterful politician writing for political purposes. We should obviously approach his words with extreme caution, but with regard to his account of his service in the Great War his words should nonetheless be studied and carefully considered, and where there is no reason to do otherwise, we should be prepared to give them weight. This is especially the case where Hitler's account can be cross referenced with other primary source accounts which you will find here. I have also relied heavily on the memoirs of those who fought alongside Hitler and where possible I have simply let them speak for themselves. Adolf Hitler was clearly not the raving lunatic of popular mythology. He was a cunning, devious and astute politician who kept his finger on the conservative pulse of Germany. Millions of ordinary Germans later fell under Hitler's spell and although anti-Semitism was rife, it was not something which was on the personal agenda of *all* conservatives in Germany, but the desire to re-build national prestige undoubtedly was. Increasingly historians have come to reassess the influence of ultra-nationalism on Hitler and in the process have come to accept the fundamental voracity of much of what you are about to read here. It is now widely accepted that the picture of Hitler as a dutiful and even brave soldier is essentially an accurate. Scholars and general readers seeking a primary insight into the early life of Adolf Hitler now have the recollections of his boyhood friend Kubizek, the recollections of his wartime comrades alongside a few recent pieces which have come to light such as Alexander Moritz Frey's account of his war time experiences with Hitler and their subsequent encounters in Munich.

Hitler's crimes against humanity are now synonymous with the fate of the Jews in Germany and throughout occupied Europe. Accordingly 'Mein Kampf' has today assumed a key place in identifying the roots of Hitler's anti-Semitism which is often depicted as his life's work. My own view is that nationalism came first with anti-Semitism following behind. 'Mein Kampf', if taken at face value, certainly seems to back up that point of view and as such forms a key part of the functionalist versus intentionalist debate. The intentionalists insist with considerable force that the infamous passage stating that if 12,000–15,000 Jews were gassed, then 'the sacrifice of millions of soldiers would not have been in vain,' proves quite clearly that Hitler had a master plan for the genocide of the Jewish people all along. Functionalist historians reject this assertion, noting that the passage does not call for the destruction of the entire Jewish people and also stress that although *'Mein Kampf'* is suffused with an extreme anti-Semitism, it is the only time in the entire book that Hitler ever explicitly refers to the murder of Jews. Given that *'Mein Kampf'* is 720 pages long, Functionalist historians caution that it may be making too much out of one sentence. It is obvious that Hitler was clearly imbued with anti-Semitism, from at least 1923, although the degree of anti-Semitic hatred contained in *'Mein Kampf'* is no greater or less than that contained in the writings and speeches of earlier *völkisch* leaders such as Wilhelm Marr, Georg Ritter von Schönerer, Houston Stewart Chamberlain and Karl Lueger, all of whom routinely called Jews a 'disease' and 'vermin'. Regardless of which school of thought we fall into, what certainly comes over loud and clear is Hitler's willingness to advocate violent and inhumane solutions to political issues. His experience in the trenches of the Great War seems to have done nothing to assuage that position.

My own view inclines towards the Functionalist historians who broadly argue that Hitler had overcome his Jewish opponents by 1935 with the introduction of the Nuremberg laws and from that point onwards his expansionist agenda was his main focus.

However, the debates stemming from Hitler's participation in the Great War continue to unfold to-day and it is important to keep an open mind. There really is no final answer and the judgement of each individual reader is as valid as the next. I trust that you will find the ideas expressed in this book compelling and persuasive but what really matters is the sum of the knowledge and our willingness to explore the past in a genuine spirit of openness.

Thank you for buying this book I sincerely hope it repays your investment in time and money.

Bob Carruthers
Edinburgh, 2014

- CHAPTER 1 -

THE DRIFTER IN VIENNA AND MUNICH

I N MAY 1913 ADOLF HITLER WAS A TWENTY-three year old living rough in Vienna; he had come to the city from his home town of Linz in order to further his aspiration to study either as an artist or an architect. Not surprisingly, for a young man with limited talent and no suitable educational qualifications, a doorway into either of his chosen careers had not materialised. After five fruitless years in the city engaged in the unsuccessful pursuit of a new life, he was embittered, destitute and homeless. The optimistic young man who aspired to a professional respectability had, by 1913, been reduced living the life of a down and out in Vienna eking out an existence by painting and selling tourist postcards. He lived in the dismal surroundings of a men's hostel at Mendlemennstrasse 27 with other itinerant men who had fallen on hard times during the great depression which gripped the whole of Austria.

Not surprisingly Hitler was shamed and degraded by the outcome of his Viennese sojourn and it is understandable that Hitler eventually came to despise the city which was the location for the worst and most humiliating experiences of his life. Moreover, under the influence of his nascent racial agenda, he came to view the bustling Austro-Hungarian capital as being entirely dominated by Slavs and Jews. For Hitler the city represented a melting pot of races, a process which Hitler later described as inexorably diluting racial purity of his precious German *völk*. According to his own account in *'Mein Kampf'* Hitler moved from Austria to Germany for what he later described as 'political' reasons. However, on all of the available evidence, it appears he may actually have moved for a combination of economic and personal reasons connected with his desire to avoid further misery; and more importantly, the looming prospect compulsory service in the Austro-Hungarian army.

For companionship during the move to Germany Hitler took with him an acquaintance named Rudolf Hausler who had also lived in the Vienna men's hostel. The pair decided against the obvious move, to the Prussian capital at Berlin, and settled instead on a move to Munich - the elegant capital of the state of Bavaria. The move to Munich got off to a good start and they soon found lodgings in the city with the family of Herr Josef Popp, a Munich master tailor. Herr Popp lived in modest circumstances, but he boasted of having travelled as far as Paris and therefore considered himself a man of the world. The Popp family lived at Schleissheimerstrasse 34 and Frau Anna Popp in particular seems to have quickly developed something of a soft spot for Hitler, the man she dubbed the 'Austrian charmer'.

Although Hitler soon developed a cordial relationship with the Popps, the business of sharing a room with Rudolf Hausler progressed somewhat less smoothly. Hausler justifiably objected to Hitler's habit of reading late into the night by the light of a smoky petrol lamp, and eventually Hausler was driven to find his own room elsewhere. Relations between the two however continued to be cordial and the pair remained close until, on the outbreak of the Great War in 1914, Hausler moved back to Vienna to enlist in the Austro-Hungarian army. Even after the war the relationship endured and Hausler later became a senior Nazi functionary in Vienna.

Despite the small hiccup with Hausler, Hitler was at last living in the embrace of what he described as a 'true city of the Reich.' The Hitler family had briefly lived in Passau in Bavaria and Hitler was happy that he was now once more living in his beloved Bavaria for the first time since his infancy. His love affair with the city of Munich was to last all of his life and he later recorded his impressions with great affection in the pages of 'Mein Kampf':

'At last I came to Munich, in the spring of 1912. The city itself was as familiar to me as if I had lived for years within its walls. This was

because my studies in architecture had been constantly turning my attention to the metropolis of German art. One must know Munich if one would know Germany, and it is impossible to acquire knowledge of German art without seeing Munich.

All things considered, this pre-war sojourn was by far the happiest and most contented time of my life. My earnings were very slender; but after all I did not live for the sake of painting. I painted in order to get the bare necessities of existence while I continued my studies. I was firmly convinced that I should finally succeed in reaching the goal I had marked out for myself. And this conviction alone was strong enough to enable me to bear the petty hardships of everyday life without worrying very much about them.'

It is important to note that Hitler claims to have moved to Munich in 1912 while all the other sources, including the Police records in Vienna, still point to him being a resident of Vienna and living in Mendlemennstrasse 27 until at least 24th May 1913. His former business associate Reinhold Hanisch[1], gives an even later date for the move and states that Hitler was still in Vienna as late as August 1913. In any event, we can be certain that it was not until 1913 that Hitler finally made the decision to leave Austria and strike out for a new life Germany.

Whatever the true date, the move to Munich was an auspicious one for Hitler who developed a renewed sense of purpose after his fruitless struggles in Vienna. That new energy was inspired by the charms of the sophisticated capital of Bavaria which Hitler later recalled in the pages of *'Mein Kampf'*:

'Moreover, almost from the very first moment of my sojourn there I came to love that city more than any other place known to me. A German city! I said to myself. How different to Vienna. It was with a feeling of disgust that my imagination reverted to that Babylon of races. Another pleasant feature here was the way the people spoke German, which was much nearer my own way of speaking than the

---

1. Hanisch's memoirs were published in America on 5th April, 1939 in the 'New Republic' magazine under the title 'I was Hitler's buddy.'

Viennese idiom. The Munich idiom recalled the days of my youth, especially when I spoke with those who had come to Munich from Lower Bavaria. There were a thousand or more things which I inwardly loved or which I came to love during the course of my stay. But what attracted me most was the marvelous wedlock of native folk-energy with the fine artistic spirit of the city, that unique harmony from the Hofbräuhaus to the Odeon, from the October Festival to the Pinakothek, etc. The reason why my heart's strings are entwined around this city as around no other spot in this world is probably because Munich is and will remain inseparably connected with the development of my own career; and the fact that from the beginning of my visit I felt inwardly happy and contented is to be attributed to the charm of the marvelous Wittelsbach Capital, which has attracted probably everybody who is blessed with a feeling for beauty instead of commercial instincts.'

In 1913 there is no question that Hitler could certainly have used a few more finely honed commercial instincts of his own. Hitler's move to Munich had been made possible, in part at least, due to his inheritance of a small legacy from his father's estate; and it would appear he also relied upon the continued support of his long suffering Aunt Johanna. Nonetheless, his small store of money was quickly exhausted and he was soon living hand to mouth once more. We know that Hitler had been a sickly youth with chest problems and it is not surprising that five years of strain and poor diet in Vienna combined with his continuing struggles in Munich left their mark on his already poor health.

Writing in the pages of *'Mein Kampf'* in 1924 Hitler markedly described his reasons for moving to Munich from Vienna as 'political', but there is a strong suspicion that the move may actually have been in search of a better life. There is certainly strong circumstantial evidence that the move was connected with Hitler's desire to avoid compulsory service in the Austro-Hungarian Habsburg Army. Hitler was a subject of the Austro-Hungarian Empire and his age group was due for compulsory military service in 1913. The suspicion that he was a draft dodger grows even stronger when one considers the passage in the book, 'The Young Hitler I Knew', by Hitler's friend August Kubizek. Kubizek recalled the time in 1911 when he himself had been called up for service and Hitler had strongly urged that his friend should flee to Germany as the best means to avoid military service in the Austro-Hungarian army.[2]

If it was indeed his intention to avoid military service by a move to Munich then Hitler had clearly not bargained on the co-operative and efficient relations between the authorities on either side of the Austro-German border. It did not take long before Hitler was tracked down by the Austrian Government. His problems were compounded when a policeman arrived at Schleissheimerstrasse 34 to inform Hitler that he was now faced with the immediate prospect of having to report for military service for the despised Habsburg Empire. If we are to accept his own account Hitler received the news of his call up very late and too late to actually report for duty in Linz as required. He urgently enlisted the help of a Munich lawyer Ernst Hepp and with the help of the Austrian embassy in Munich he was narrowly able to avoid being branded as a deserter. Hitler and Hepp quickly set to work and were successful in their aim of obtaining dispensation for Hitler to report late and to attend for his medical in nearby Salzburg rather than distant Linz. Having obtained that official sanction, Hitler seems to have finally resigned himself to his fate, and in February 1914, he dutifully rushed back to Salzburg ready to do his military service.

Fortunately from Hitler's point of view the debilitating effects of his years of struggle in Vienna, combined with his poor health record, were readily apparent. He failed his medical examination and, by this stroke of fortune, was lucky enough to be spared Austrian military service.

It is important to note that Hitler escaped on entirely legitimate grounds by virtue of the fact that he was deemed physically unfit for the peace-time army. In later years the circumstances surrounding Hitler's call up for service in the Austro-Hungarian army would take

---

2. The book went through various incarnations both during the Third Reich and afterwards. It is not considered a completely reliable source but may be substantially relied upon in most respects.

on enormous significance for him and would lead to a series of scornful gibes being levelled at Hitler by his political opponents who claimed, with some justification, that he was a 'draft dodger' on the run from the Austro-Hungarian Army. What was less convincing was his opponents claim that he had been somehow unwillingly enlisted into the ranks of the Bavarian army.

Due to the overwhelming strength of the circumstantial evidence Hitler could not risk a fight with those newspapers which habitually referred to him as an Austrian draft dodger. Finally however, in 1932, the SDP supporting newspaper *'Echo Der Woche'* stepped over the mark by mistakenly labelling him a 'deserter' from the Austrian army. Hitler knew this was untrue and in order to protect his precarious reputation, he was able to take court action against the newspaper safe in the knowledge that he could not lose on this narrow definition of the literal truth. With the help of the testimony of his former colleagues Hitler easily won his court case. The evidence however had to stand up to the full scrutiny of the law and Hitler was able to produce incontestable evidence in the form of an official statement from the Austrian authorities:

Office of the State Government, State Registry Office, Nr. 786
Official Statement
  Adolf Hitler, born on 20 April 1889 in Braunau is Inn and resident of Linz, Upper Austria, son of Alois and Klara (maiden name, Pötzl), was found by examination of the 3rd age group in Salzburg on 5 February 1914 to be "too weak for military or support service," and was declared "unfit for military service."

Linz, 23 February 1932,
signed Ovitz[3]

There are many grey areas concerning the facts behind the life of Adolf Hitler, but in this one instance at least, we can be certain of

---

3. The statement was later published in the 1932 pamphlet entitled *'Tatsachen und Lügen um Hitler'* (Facts and Lies About Adolf Hitler), this pamphlet was published in Munich in the wake of the 1932 court case.

what happened. Adolf Hitler dutifully reported himself to the military authorities at Salzburg, on 5th February 1914, but was found to be unfit *(zu schwach)* for military service. We can be confident therefore that it was a relieved, and no doubt surprised, Adolf Hitler who returned to Munich in February 1914. His lodgings at Schleissheimerstrasse 34 were still available to him and his unremarkable life continued much as before; until in August 1914 world events conspired to change the course of his life forever.

- CHAPTER 2 -

HITLER AND THE LIST REGIMENT

W E KNOW FROM HIS OWN ACCOUNT that Adolf Hitler delighted in the prospect of war in his lifetime. In the pages of *'Mein Kampf'* he declared himself thoroughly disappointed by the fact that he had been born into a period of lasting peace. Somewhat bizarrely he confesses that he yearned for war and actually rued the fact that, during his own boyhood, the world was relatively peaceful with no major armed conflict taking place. However that situation was soon to change, to Hitler's lasting delight the spectre of war loomed eventually in South Africa and he avidly followed events from afar:

'Then the Boer War came, like a glow of lightning on the far horizon. Day after day I used to gaze intently at the newspapers and I almost 'devoured' the telegrams and communiques, overjoyed to think that I could witness that heroic struggle, even though from so great a distance. When the Russo-Japanese War came I was older and better able to judge for myself. For national reasons I then took the side of the Japanese in our discussions. I looked upon the defeat of the Russians as a blow to Austrian Slavism.'

By 1913, like so many others, Hitler sensed that a European war was almost inevitable and he later confessed that, as an Austrian subject, what he had feared most was that Germany would become involved in a conflict which did not affect Austria. In such an event it was Hitler's great fear that the Austrian State, for domestic political reasons, would not come to the aid of her ally:

'Many years had passed between that time and my arrival in

Munich. I now realized that what I formerly believed to be a morbid decadence was only the lull before the storm.'

In 1934, after Hitler had become Chancellor of Germany, the writer and party member Heinz A. Heinz was authorised by the Nazi party to interview those who had known Hitler during his wilderness years in the lead up to the Great War. The results of these interviews were published for foreign consumption in book form under the title 'Germany's Hitler' which first appeared in 1934. Building on those interviews Heinz was able to describe the scenes around Munich in 1914. By then the population of Europe were already aware that they were sitting on a powder keg. The complex series of European alliances between the great powers, all pointed in one dismal direction - war. Heinz, writing with many dramatic flourishes, including the verbatim quotes and copious exclamation marks which mark German writing of the period, described the circumstances in which Hitler found himself in the run up to the outbreak of the long anticipated European war:

'It was in his lodgings at Frau Popp's that the young student painter first heard of the shot at Sarajevo. There was a tremendous babble going on suddenly outside; in the street below people came running together; a word floated up to his ears, and on his going down presently to find out what the commotion was all about… Thus Frau Popp, breathless with excitement, "Der osterreichische Thronfolger Erzherzog Franz Ferdinand ist ermordet worden!" (The Austrian heir, Archduke Franz Ferdinand, has been assassinated!)

Hitler pushed past her into the street. Thrusting his way into a press of people, staring open-mouthed at a placard, he read the announcement of the crime for himself. The perpetrators, it seemed, had already been arrested.'

Heinz goes on to state that 'the whole world gasped at the news.' No one in Munich required to be particularly well posted as to the political situation just then to realise that this must mean an explosion in the Balkans. The Wittelsbachs, the Bavarian royal family, had received the unfortunate Archduke and his wife as recently as March 1913, and they certainly foresaw great political consequences of a war between Austria and Russia, which would pre-sage the World War.

Heinz also recalled how the city of Munich seethed with indignation and in Vienna, too, the mood was angry and there were flashpoints all over the city as mobs threatened the Serbian Legation. This murder was understood to have been the overt act of a conspiracy which Austria-Hungary suspected to have its origin in Serbia. The bomb throwers at Sarajevo, and Princip, the man who shot the Archduke, were viewed as emissaries of Serb secret societies whose aim was dissolution of the Dual Austro-Hungarian Monarchy and the establishment of a pan-Serb State. The popular conjecture was that all of this was to be achieved with the assistance of France and England who were bent on hampering Germany's economic expansion.

Hitler was a man who devoured newspapers and he could therefore grasp the impending consequences better than Frau Popp. There followed a few days of high tension, then, on Saturday 1st August 1914, in response to the news of Russian mobilisation, came what Heinz described as the 'reluctant' Imperial order for the mobilisation of Germany's great war machine. For Adolf Hitler, what he described as 'the most memorable period' of his life had now begun. Faced with the prospect of that mighty conflict, it seemed to him that all of his past fell away into oblivion. With a wistful pride, Hitler, in the pages of 'Mein Kampf', looked back on the days of war with a warm enthusiasm and a delight that fortune had permitted him the honour of taking his place in that 'heroic struggle.'

Ironically, the Sarajevo flashpoint and the outbreak of war with Serbia made it certain that the Austria-Hungarian Empire would indeed be involved in fighting side by side with Germany. For Hitler, the outbreak of war which married Germany and Austria-Hungary as allies in which he could take part as a soldier fighting for the Kaiser, was a deliverance from the distress that had weighed upon him during his long sojourn in Vienna:

> 'I am not ashamed to acknowledge today that I was carried away
> by the enthusiasm of the moment and that I sank down upon my

knees and thanked Heaven out of the fullness of my heart for the
favour of having been permitted to live in such a time.'

Hitler appears to have been correct in forming his view that the Great War was certainly not forced on the masses; the outbreak of war seems to have been conjured into existence almost as if it were the subject of a popular demand. For Hitler it appeared as if there was a common desire to bring what he called 'the general feeling of uncertainty' to an end once and for all. He was intensely proud of how more than two million German males voluntarily joined the colours, ready to shed the last drop of their blood for the cause. Although even Hitler had to concede, in keeping with the western allies, the German people did not have the slightest conception of how long the war might last. People dreamed of the soldiers being home by Christmas and that then they would resume their daily work in peace. Had they known the awful truth, the universal mood of optimism would have been far less bullish.

In 1914 the state of Bavaria still maintained its own standing army, however, in the event of war, the Bavarian army formed a component part of the Imperial German Army. As such the Bavarian army took its marching orders from Prussia and, although it still maintained its own recruiting and logistical systems based in Munich, it came firmly under the direct control of Berlin. On the outbreak of war the ageing Prince-Regent Ludwig III, remained at the Residenz in Munich. His son, Crown Prince Rupprecht, however, departed for the Front where he was to serve with distinction as a senior Imperial German Army commander. Rupprecht's brother Prince Ludwig Ferdinand, at once presented himself for a military surgeon, while his sister, Princess Pilar, became a nurse.

The streets of Munich were now filled with field-grey uniforms and there was a corresponding surge of military activity. According to Heinz the enthusiastic spirit of war filled the state of Bavaria:

'Youth everywhere was sanguine and high-spirited. The sense of
war flew to everybody's head like wine. There were processions and
great cheering. If peasants called to the colours from the Bayerischer
Wald, the mountains and the Franconian plains scarcely knew what

it was all about, they only needed to learn that the Fatherland was threatened, to become as conspicuous for their enthusiasm at this moment as later they were to become conspicuous for bravery.'

Every day it seemed troops were moving off for the front. There were enormous parades as the companies massed in great open spaces and swore their oath of allegiance anew; the priests and bishops of the Protestant and Catholic churches blessed their departure; the trumpeters sounded the *Zum Gebet*; and to the accompaniment of blood-stirring martial music, and the tumultuous leave-taking of the townsfolk, masses of men entrained for the Front. Day after day crowds assembled in dense thousands before the Feldherrnhalle on the Odeonsplatz and burst into *'Die Wacht am Rhein.'* The normally reserved student painter from Vienna joined the crowds and sang along with them as lustily as the rest.

It is no surprise therefore that Hitler was part of the cheering crowd on Munich's Odeonsplatz photographed by Heinrich Hoffman on Sunday 2nd August 1914. In the famous photograph Hitler can be clearly seen waving his hat enthusiastically and welcoming the news that war had been declared on Russia the day before. Even more momentous news was to follow as France and Britain both entered the fray over the next few days. At the outbreak of the First World War, unlike his friend Hausler, Hitler did not return to Austria. He had successfully, and entirely legitimately, evaded military service for the Habsburgs and he intended to keep it that way. Hitler later recalled how he had often longed for the occasion to prove that his enthusiasm for pan-German national ideal was not 'mere vapouring.' He now felt a proud almost religious sense of joy at the prospect of being able to take the ultimate test of loyalty on the field of combat in the service of the German Reich.

No sooner had the Munich crowd begun to disperse than Hitler, the recent Austro-Hungarian reject, volunteered for service in the Bavarian army. According to the account published by Heinz, Adolf Hitler rushed upstairs to his 'studio' in the Popp apartment and dashed off an application to the *Kabinettskanzlei* of the Prince Regent for permission to enlist in a Bavarian Regiment which, in time of war, fought within the framework of the Imperial German Army. Hitler's own version of events appears in *'Mein Kampf'*, and he tells us that, immensely to his astonishment and jubilation, the very next day brought the answer. The *Herr Kabinettschef* of the Prince-Regent Ludwig III accepted the young Austrian's proffer of service, and directed him to report himself immediately at the nearest barracks. Hitler records that he fell on his knees and thanked God. His reaction seems to have been typical of the passionate enthusiasm of those first few weeks of the War with high-spirited, patriotic, untried youth debouching on every Front.

Despite having been declared unfit for Austro-Hungarian service only the year before, Hitler, although he was not even a German national, had somehow succeeded in obtaining permission to join the List Regiment (later known as 16th Bavarian Reserve Infantry Regiment, or the 16th RIR for short). Hitler later explained his reasons for making his direct appeal to the Price Regent:

'I had left Austria principally for political reasons. What therefore could be more rational than that I should put into practice the logical consequences of my political opinions, now that the war had begun. I had no desire to fight for the Habsburg cause, but I was prepared to die at any time for my own kinsfolk and the Empire to which they really belonged. On 3rd August 1914, I presented an urgent petition to His Majesty, King Ludwig III, requesting to be allowed to serve in a Bavarian regiment. In those days the Chancellery had its hands quite full and therefore I was all the more pleased when I received the answer a day later, that my request had been granted. I opened the document with trembling hands; and no words of mine could now describe the satisfaction I felt on reading that I was instructed to report to a Bavarian regiment. Within a few days I was wearing that uniform which I was not to put away again for nearly six years.'

Initially the uniform which was issued to Hitler did not represent the characteristic German uniform of 1914. There were insufficient *pickelhaube* helmets to equip the new battalion, and the recruits of the List Regiment had to be issued with the old style peaked oilcloth caps (*Landsturmmuetzen*) of the very same design as those worn during the

1812 War of Liberation and very similar to those worn by the British Expeditionary Force in 1914. This unfortunate item was to cause the List Regiment great difficulty and a number of casualties during the early battles of 1914. Despite the problems with supply of standard head-gear however, there were at least sufficient uniforms to go round and Hitler received his *feldgrau* tunic. The greenish-grey issue jacket was universal in the Imperial German Army and distinguished from the other regiments by having the regimental number 'RIR 16' sown in red onto the epaulettes. Another item of uniform equipment which was issued was a thick leather belt worn around the waist of the uniform jacket; the uniform was completed by a feldgrau trouser on which a red stripe was sown down the outside of the leg. The trousers were then tucked into the famous leather 'jack' boots to complete the look of a 1914 soldier in the service of the Kaiser.

On the surface Hitler's decision to enlist as a soldier in the ranks of the Bavarian army was a typically perverse action. After all, he had apparently gone to great lengths only six months previously to avoid military service. Hitler had now joined up on the instant as *Kriegsfreiwilliger* (war-time volunteer), and to his obvious delight found himself properly enrolled as Infanterist Number 148 in the 1st Company of the List Regiment.

The explanation to this apparent conundrum however lies in Hitler's life long political support for the pan-German nationalist *Grossdeutschsland lossung* (greater German solution). Hitler's own attitude towards the conflict was simple and clear. He believed that it was no longer a case of Austria fighting to get satisfaction from Serbia, but rather a case of the wider German peoples fighting for their own future existence. His fevered imagination pictured the Germanic lands hemmed in by enemies on all sides and furthermore entirely without the opportunity to expand horizons by overseas colonization. It was on this flimsy basis that Hitler, and so many others in 1914, surmised that it was necessary for the survival of the German Empire that Germany must assert herself in Europe by force of arms. Hitler was certainly anxious to play his part in a struggle with which he could empathise, but he wanted to play the precise part that suited him; and that meant service in the Imperial German Army not the hated Austro-Hungarian Army with its Slav influences.

For better or worse the pan-German nationalist Adolf Hitler was now firmly enrolled as a war-time volunteer number 148 in the 1st Company of the List Regiment. This formation was one of nearly 800 or so regiments to serve in the Imperial German Army on the Western Front in the Great War. In common with the other recruits, Hitler had only one worry during those optimistic early war days. He harboured a fear that his regiment might arrive too late for the fighting at the front. Every announcement of a victorious engagement produced an increasing concern, which further increased as the news of further victories arrived. Hitler wanted to see action, he was soon to get his wish - and he would not be found lacking.

In the meantime Hitler's regiment then began a short but intensive basic training program, which was held in the premises of a large public school on the Elizabethplatz in Munich.

A fellow recruit was Hans Mend, who was to play a major role in the story of Private Hitler's War. Mend was an extremely colourful character who had convictions for fraud. In 1930 when Hitler was on the brink of power, Mend published his account of his service alongside Hitler entitled *'Adolf Hitler Im Felde 1914-1918'* (Adolf Hitler At War 1914-1918) it was essentially a hagiography, but there were elements of the book which were critical of the character of Adolf Hitler. Initially it seems the book found a measure of favour with the Nazi party, but once Hitler had attained power it was disowned and supressed, all unsold copies were ordered to be withdrawn and pulped and all library shelves were cleared of the book. Like Reinhold Hanisch, Mend had come to an irrevocable breach with Hitler and despite a belated attempt to join the Nazi party, Mend was consigned to a concentration camp before dying of natural causes in the early 1940's. Mend's account is exaggerated and self-serving, it must therefore be treated with extreme caution. However, it is nonetheless written by someone who did actually serve with Hitler, and there is no reason to doubt every single word. Mend claims that he first noticed Hitler during the time the regiment was in training in Munich and tells us he first took Hitler to be an 'academic', of whom there were many in the List Regiment. Mend was struck by the manner in which Hitler lavished attention of his newly issued rifle:

'I saw him for the second time on another day, as he pottered about with his rifle. He regarded it with the delight of a woman with her jewelry, while I secretly laughed to myself.'

On the Exerzierplatz of Munich, Hitler and the List regiment embarked on a period of intensive training, with the focus on the usual exercises consisting of army drills, learning how to march in step, form fours, file evolutions, route marching and bayonet practice. What was missing was the time to develop the rank and file into proficient marksmen, and this deficiency was to come home to haunt the List Regiment when it came face to face with the highly trained British regulars who were trained in the art of marksmanship and could deliver a much high rate of accurate and sustained rifle fire.

On 8th September 1914 the men were gathered together to hear the 49 year-old commander of the List Regiment, Colonel Julius von List, address his recruits. Their commander was well aware that training time was ridiculously short, his words were preserved for posterity in the Official Regimental history by Franz Rubenbauer:

'Comrades! I welcome with all my heart and full confidence all officers, doctors, and officials, all Offiziersstellvertreter, NCOs, and troops. Our Regiment, whose men for the most part are untrained, is expected to be ready for mobile deployment within a few weeks. This is a difficult task, but with the admirable spirit which animates all members of this regiment, not an impossible one... With God's blessing, let's begin our work for Kaiser, King, and Fatherland!' [4]

Hitler and the Listers were not destined to remain in Munich barracks for long and on 7th October 1914 he found the time to bid a fond farewell to the family of the tailor, Josef Popp. Frau Popp later recalled how he requested that, in the event of his death, the Popp family should write to his sister on his behalf and suggest that she might

---

4. See Thomas Weber 'Hitler's First War', p19.

perhaps like to receive his few possessions. According to Frau Popp he then informed the Popps that, in the event that Paula did not wish to have his property, then the Popps were free to dispose of them as they wished. Frau Popp wept, and after shaking hands with Josef, Hitler took his leave and embarked on his 'great adventure.' [5]

On 8th October 1914 the recruits took their Oaths and swore allegiance to Kaiser Wilhelm II but also to King Ludwig III of Bavaria, and to Hitler's own monarch: Kaiser Franz Josef. Standing next to Hitler was Ernst Schmidt, who would become Hitler's closest wartime companion. Schmidt was another List veteran who would later write his own hagiography which was more acceptable to Hitler. Schmidt noticed Hitler's extraordinary appetite; he would not be the last to comment on the voracious appetite of the slender Austrian:

'On the day of the swearing-in, there was a double-ration of roast pork and potato salad. Hitler told me several times that the festive day remained particularly pleasant in his memory, as he was always hungry. During the war he was known for being always hungry, and could become ill when the food supply was delayed.'

With the men sworn in, the List Regiment was ordered to prepare to march off for a few weeks further training at Lechfeld, a pleasant town at the confluence of the Lech and the Danube about seventy miles west of Munich. Here the wide river meadows provided ideal terrain for the divisional training exercises which were to follow as the List Regiment combined with three other Regiments to form the 6th Bavarian Reserve Division (6th BRD). The men were all glad of the change, and left the city, after a tremendous send-off from the populace, still anxious that they might not be afforded the opportunity to come to grips with the enemy before the War was over. Adolf Hitler recalled his memories of these halcyon days in the pages of *'Mein Kampf'*:

'As the scene unfolds itself before my mind, it seems only like yesterday. I see myself among my young comrades on our first parade drill, and so on until at last the day came on which we were to leave

---

5. Frau Popp was interviewed and quoted in 'Germany's Hitler' by Heinz A. Heinz.

for the front. In common with the others, I had one worry during those days. This was a fear that we might arrive too late for the fighting at the front. Time and again that thought disturbed me; and every announcement of a victorious engagement left a bitter taste, which increased as the news of further victories arrived.'

On Saturday 9th October, the 1st Company of the 16th Bavarian Reserve Infantry including Adolf Hitler in its ranks set off on foot for Lechfeld, and began the long march which would take them seventy miles west of Munich to the confluence of the rivers Lech and the Danube. Burdened by the weight of the full packs on their backs, they marched off in pouring rain which continued for the next eleven hours. Not surprisingly, Hitler found the march hard going and he voiced his frustrations in the letter he wrote to Frau Popp on 20th October 1914:

'We were on our feet from 6.30 A.M. to 5 P.M. and during the march we took part in a major exercise, all of this in constant rain I was put up in a stable, soaked through and through. There was no possibility of sleep.'

The next day the company continued their march to Lechfeld on what was described as a bitterly cold Sunday, they marched for thirteen hours before bivouacking in the open for the night. Finally, on 11th October 1914, Hitler and the rest of the 1st Company reached Lechfeld in mid afternoon. The regiment was to receive no respite after its gruelling march and immediately embarked upon a programme of further training.

Franz Rubenhauer, an officer of the List regiment who was later to produce the bulk of the material for the regimental history, recalled the detail of their activities:

'We still gratefully remember the warm welcome we received from the local population, in the places where we had our living quarters, after the exhausting daily exercises on the vast Lechfeld, or from the practice firing range in the meadows of the Lech, singing marching songs with high and clear voices; old and young were out and about and marched with us. After we were dismissed for the day, they took

us back into their homes, where the food waited ready for us on their stoves.'

While they honed their skills at Lechfeld, the List Regiment did not have too long to worry about missing out on the war. Their rapid, and wholly inadequate, bout of basic training in Munich and Lechfeld was now drawing to a close and the day duly arrived when the List Regiment departed on active war service.

On 20th October, Hitler wrote to Frau Popp, bringing her up to date on all that had happened to him since he departed Munich and informing her that he would soon be moving out for the front:

'We are going on a four-day journey, probably to Belgium. I am tremendously excited... After arrival at our destination I will write immediately and give you my address. I hope we get to England.'

The fresh warriors of the List Regiment now boarded a troop train which headed north and west and, just as Hitler had hoped, they soon deduced that their fate was indeed to fight on the Western Front. During the Great War, the Russian Front was regarded as the softer option and Hitler would no doubt have been very happy in the realization that the List Regiment was destined to see action where the fighting was hardest. As the train continued its journey north and westwards, Hitler, for the first time in his life, saw the Rhine river. The magical music and narrative of the mighty Ring of the Nibelung cycle of operas by Richard Wagner had long been an inspiration to Hitler. As the regiment journeyed westwards, Hitler recalled a dramatic episode when the first soft rays of the morning sun broke through the light mist and revealed the gigantic Niederwald Statue. Hitler described the powerful moment when with one accord the whole troop train broke into the strains of *'Die Wacht Am Rhein'* at which point Hitler emotionally declared that his heart was 'fit to burst'.

In later years former Private Ignatz Westenkirchner, another of Hitler's List comrades, was also interviewed by Heinz A. Heinz, the Nazi propagandist who was commissioned to write a biography of Hitler entitled 'Germany's Hitler' which appeared in the Thirties. Heinz described his first impressions of Herr Ignaz Westenkirchner, who at that stage was an ex-service man, and former war-time comrade of the Führer. He was, in 1934, thanks to the influence of Adolf Hitler, employed on the *Völkischer Beobachter*, the official Nazi newspaper based in Munich:

'A somewhat small-built man, this Ignaz Westenkirchner, thin, with a clean-shaven face much lined and worn, and, of course, somewhere about the Führer's own age. He wore a simple blue suit and had a regular galaxy of various-coloured pencils sticking out of the pocket in his jacket. He had a job in the dispatching department of the paper, hence the multi-coloured pencils. He received the writer in the waiting-room of the offices of the Völkischer Beobachter in Munich. But we repaired immediately to a quieter room where we could talk in comfort. 'Dear me, yes,' said he, 'the Führer remains ever the good comrade that he was! you shall have the whole account of our doings on the Western Front....'

The Führer himself also touched upon of his War experiences in *'Mein Kampf'*, but it is a brief version which concentrates heavily on the events of October 1914, so we are lucky to have Herr Westenkirchner's verbatim story as told to Heinz. No doubt refreshed by the very similar passage in *'Mein Kampf'*, as Westenkirchner began to unfold his story to Heinz A. Heinz he described the excitement of the journey to Flanders in almost identical terms to Hitler's description:

'We were all in topping spirits that day, our heads stuffed with no end of war nonsense, sure as eggs is eggs the glorious fighting would be all over by Christmas or the New Year at latest. We reached the Rhine that night. Lots of us south Bavarian chaps had never seen the Rhine before, and then in the dawn, I remember as if it were yesterday, how it just struck us all to see the sun drawing up the mist from the river and unveiling before our dazzled eyes that splendid statue of Germania which looks down from the Niederwald. How we yelled the 'Wacht am Rhein', the whole lot of us for the first time going out to war.'

The journey to the front for Hitler may have been something of a mythical pageant with Wagnerian overtones, but as they neared the front the grim realities of the first of the modern wars gradually enveloped the enthusiastic volunteers. The infantry tactics of August 1914 had not kept pace with the advances in artillery and machine guns. The result was to be the 'slaughter of the innocents' which produced a huge German casualty toll as flesh met steel in Flanders.

- CHAPTER 3 -

THE BATTLE FOR GHELUVELT

THE LIST REGIMENT WERE AT LAST ON their way to war, but even with modern transportation systems the problem of moving such an enormous mass of men and material placed a terrific strain on the rail system and Ignatz Westenkirchner recalled the frustrations of the latter stages of the slow and tortuous journey to the front:

'It took us two days to reach Lille as our train only crawled from that point onward. Across war-ravaged Belgium we provided reinforcements for the 6th Bavarian Division of the Army of the Crown Prince Rupprecht. The great battles of the Marne and the Aisne were over by this time; Antwerp had fallen; the first phase of the Battle of Ypres in which the Allied enemy had made every effort to effect a great turning movement round our right flank, clearing the Belgian coast line, and forcing us out of Bruges and Ghent, had failed.'

Writing in the regimental history of the List Regiment Franz Rubenhauer recalled the arrival of the regiment in Lille:

'On the morning of 23rd October 1914 between 7 and 9 o'clock, our troops arrived in Lille. There had been lengthy delays. For long hours the trains stood immobile at open stretches, then crawled forward from station to station at a snail's pace of 8 kilometers per hour. After a few hours, as Lille approached, unbroken cannon fire was heard in the Westerly direction of Armentièeres, fliers were seen circling in the brightly illuminated sky - one already felt the vicinity of the Front.'

Hitler's regiment de-trained and marched into Lille. This was the first time Hitler had ever travelled beyond the borders of German-speaking territories. Stopping at the courtyard of the Old Stock Exchange, the men were ordered to sleep on the hard flagstones for the night after which they halted in Lille for four days and the scene was recorded in the diary of the List Regiment's chaplain, Father Norbert, a somewhat eccentric figure who habitually dressed in a monk's habit:

'Lille, and in particular the central station, was a terrible sight. The entire train station was a shambles. The wounded lay everywhere. 1,200 houses were said to have been destroyed in the bombardment, most of them grandiose buildings. There were burnt-out gables and smoking piles of rubble everywhere, along with crying and begging women and children, and withdrawn, sullen men. In the military hospitals, of which there are fifteen in the city, lie about 4,000 soldiers, most of them seriously wounded, but no clergymen; the French priests are not allowed to visit the injured due to fear of espionage. Because the enemy received intelligence from the church tower, through signs and the chiming of the hour and the direction of the hand, the clergymen were arrested and were not allowed to enter the rectory again.... My accoutrements - or monk's habit - excited everywhere a great commotion amongst friends and foe alike. I was even to be arrested as a spy, as a result of my dress. For five hours I was closely watched by a constable and 15 men, until the mistake was cleared up.'

In addition to the Popp family Hitler was also in correspondence with Herr Ernst Hepp, the Munich lawyer who had previously represented Hitler in his troubles with the Austrian government over his failure to report for military service. It provides a revealing insight into the affairs of the List Regiment from Hitler's contemporary viewpoint. In a letter written in February 1915 Hitler recalled for Herr Hepp in some detail the circumstances in the lead up to the early engagements:

'After a really lovely journey down the Rhine, we reached Lille on 23rd October. We could already see the effects of the war as we travelled through Belgium. We saw the conflagrations of war and heard its ferocious winds. As far as Douai, our journey was reasonably safe and quiet. Then came shock after shock. In some places, the base artillery had been destroyed in spite of the strongest

defense. We were now frequently coming upon blown up bridges and wrecked locomotives. Although the train kept going at a snail's pace, we encountered more and more horrors: graves. Then in the distance we heard our heavy guns.

'Toward evening we arrived in Lille, which was knocked about rather a lot in the suburbs. We got off the train and hung about around our stacked rifles, and shortly before midnight we were on the march; and at last we entered the town. It was an endless monotonous road left and right with miserable workmen's dwellings, and the countryside blackened with smoke. The pavements were poor and bad and dirty. There were no signs of any inhabitants, and there was no one on the street after 9 P.M. except the military. We were almost in danger of our lives - because the place was so full of guns and ammunition carts - and through them, we eventually reached the Citadel. We spent the night in the courtyard of the stock exchange building. This pretentious building was not yet completed. We had to lie down with full packs, and were kept at the ready. It was very cold on the stone pavement and we could not sleep. The next day we changed our quarters, and this time we were in a very large glass building. There was no lack of fresh air, the iron framework was still standing, and the panes of glass had been smashed into millions of fragments in the German bombardment. During the day, something more was attempted. We inspected the town and, most of all, we admired the tremendous military equipment; and all of Lille lay open, the gigantic shapes of the town rolling before our astonished eyes. At night there was singing, and for me it was the last time.'

The time for the List Regiment to engage in action was fast approaching and on the 27th October at 1:00 A.M., shortly before they were due to march off to the front, Hitler's regiment was mustered in the Place de Concert, to hear an 'Order of the Day' by the Bavarian Crown Prince Rupprecht who railed against the Englishmen opposing them.

'We have now the fortune to have the Englishmen on our front, the troops of that people whose antagonism has been at work for so many years in order to surround us with a ring of enemies and strangle us.

We have to thank them above all for this bloody, terrible war.... when you meet up with this enemy, demonstrate to them that the German cannot be swept so lightly from world history, show them through German blows of a quite special kind. Here is the enemy who stands most in the way of the restoration of peace. Onwards!'

Hitler was full of patriotic fervour and he was eager for the fight and every detail of his new world was to be savoured. The Hepp letter continued the narrative of the lead up to the fight at Gheluvelt:

'On the third night, about 2 A.M., there was a sudden alarm and, about 3 A.M., we marched away in full marching order from the assembly point. No one knew for certain why we were marching, but in any case we regarded it as an exercise. It was rather a dark night, and we had hardly been marching for twenty minutes when we turned left and met two columns of cavalry and other troops, and the road was so blocked there was no room for us.'

Ignatz Westenkirchner also recalled the build-up to the first engagement which formed part of a larger offensive which was known to the British as the First Battle of Ypres and to the Germans as Langemark:

'We had established a line to the sea (Nieuport), and we Bavarians amongst the rest coming up in time for the great offensive of the 31st of October and the 1st of November, when for forty-eight hours two and a half German Army Corps stormed the Wytschaete Messines Ridge, saw the beginning of the second phase of that enormous struggle. From Lille where we put in perhaps half a day we proceeded by train again to a place called Ledeghem, but after that it was all marching. Now we were within earshot of the guns: the thunder on the Front became even nearer. The country seemed awfully flat and monotonous; the only villages we passed were nothing but heaps of gaping ruins. Dead horses blown up like balloons lay in the ditches. We got the stench of them. We went through places called Dadizeele and Terhan, and approached Becelaere, a half-demolished village, the centre of the enemy's First Division.'

On 29th October 1914 the List Regiment was temporarily attached to the 54th Reserve Division, and it was with this division that the untried men of the regiment experienced their first action. They were sent forward to relieve a hard-pressed Württemburg unit and took some casualties as a result of their non-standard *Landsturmmuetzen* head gear which so closely resembled the British 1914 pattern caps. Hans Mend was engaged as a runner in the thick of the action and he recalled the devastating effect of the rounds fired by the men on his own side who were under the mistaken impression that the Listers were British troops.

> *'We reached Becalaere and were immediately in action and already this first day endured enormous losses. Since the troops of the List Regiment had received as headgear with their equipment militia caps the Würtemmburgers, in the belief that they were English, had fired violently on them, through this error many had to lose their lives.'*

With English and Belgian shells falling all around, the battle continued for three days, with fierce causalities on both sides. Hitler and the 1st Company advanced and retreated into a storm of fire four times until eventually the village of Gheluvelt finally fell into German hands. Ignatz Westenkirchner was also present at the action and his account closely matches the description which appears in *'Mein Kampf'*: [6]

> *'Here the fire was intensely hot. We advanced in the face of a bombardment. It was already night, cold and wet. We came well within range, scrambling over the muddy broken ground, taking whatever shelter we could behind hedges, in ditches and in shell-holes, our way lit by the glare of houses burning like torches in the lurid blackness, and fell at last upon the enemy, in a hand-to-hand fight, man to man, fiercely thrusting with our bayonets.'*

The task for the 1st Company of the List Regiment was to take up positions just to the north of the main road to Ypres and to co-operate with the Württembergers and other elements of the 54th Reserve Division in order to capture the village and open the road to Ypres. The chateau of Gheluveldt village was captured by the Listers but fell back

---

6. Hitler's *'Mein Kampf'* was officially translated in 1936 by James Murphy and it is this version which is quoted here.

into the hands of the British after a ferocious counter attack by the men of the Worcester Regiment. We are fortunate that we also have Adolf Hitler's letter to Ernst Hepp which provides us with a surprisingly detailed account of the reality of service in a front-line unit during the early months of the Great War.

'Then morning came. We were now a long way from Lille. The thunder of gunfire had grown somewhat stronger. Our column moved forward like a giant snake. At 9 A.M., we halted in the park of a country house. We had two hours' rest and then moved on again, marching until 8 P.M. We no longer moved as a regiment, but split up into companies, each man taking cover against enemy airplanes. At 9 P.M., we pitched camp. I couldn't sleep. Four paces from my bundle of straw lay a dead horse. The animal was already half decayed. Finally, a German howitzer battery immediately behind us kept sending two shells flying over our heads into the darkness of the night every quarter of an hour. They came whistling and hissing through the air, and then, far in the distance, there came two dull thuds. We all listened. None of us had ever heard that sound before. While we were huddled close together, whispering softly and looking up at the stars in the heavens, a terrible racket broke out in the distance. At first it was a long way off, and then the crackling came closer and closer, and the sound of single shells grew to a multitude, finally becoming a continuous roar. All of us felt the blood quickening in our veins. The English were making one of their night attacks. We waited a long time, uncertain what was happening. Then it grew quieter and at last the sound ceased altogether - except for our own batteries - which sent out their iron greetings to the night every quarter of an hour. In the morning we found a big shell hole. We had to brush ourselves up a bit, and about 10 A.M. there was another alarm and, a quarter of an hour later, we were on the march. After a long period of wandering about we reached a farm that had been shot to pieces and we camped here. I was on watch duty that night and, about one o'clock, we suddenly had another alarm; and we marched off at three o'clock in the morning. We had just taken a bit of food,

and we were waiting for our marching orders, when Major Count Zech rode up: "Tomorrow we are attacking the English!" he said. So it had come at last! We were all overjoyed; and after making this announcement, the Major went on foot to the head of the column.'

The 'English' which Major Count Zech was referring to consisted of elements of Worcester Regiment in position between the village of Gheluvelt and the town of Ypres. Also in the vicinity were some companies of the Scottish regular regiment, the renowned Black Watch. Although this was not a full scale battle it was to prove a bitterly fought encounter. Hitler only ever fought in two engagements and, not surprisingly, the events of October and early 1914 were destined to feature heavily in the pages of *'Mein Kampf'*.

The List Regiment had well and truly received it's baptism of fire on 29th October 1914 and the casualties suffered by the List regiment in October 1914 were severe. Hitler's description of the regiment's first taste of combat reads like political hyperbole; until we compare it to the other accounts of the fighting all of which confirm the ferocity of the engagement:

'And then followed a damp, cold night in Flanders. We marched in silence throughout the night and as the morning sun came through the mist an iron greeting suddenly burst above our heads. Shrapnel exploded in our midst and spluttered in the damp ground. But before the smoke of the explosion disappeared a wild 'Hurrah' was shouted from two hundred throats, in response to this first greeting of Death. Then began the whistling of bullets and the booming of cannons, the shouting and singing of the combatants. With eyes straining feverishly, we pressed forward, quicker and quicker, until we finally came to close-quarter fighting, there beyond the beet-fields and the meadows. Soon the strains of a song reached us from afar. Nearer and nearer, from company to company, it came. And while Death began to make havoc in our ranks we passed the song on to those beside us: Deutschland, Deutschland Über Alles, Über Alles In Der Welt.'

Hitler and the List Regiment aquitted themselves well during the fight around Gheluvelt, but casualties, amounting to two thirds of the strength of the regiment, were very high - even by Great War standards. Hans Mend, who had since become Colonel List's personal messenger, described the battle on the morning of the first day as: 'a last awakening for many of my comrades.' Mend reported that the skies were flaming red from the burning villages as they marched towards their first battle and claimed that he clearly recalled the figure of Adolf Hitler near the head of the regiment bent forward and with a smile on his lips. Mend tells us that he wondered to himself how this slightly built man would manage if he had to carry a full field pack. However Mend would later revise his estimate of Hitler who seems to have overcome his early health problems and proved himself to be made of the right stuff for the life of a soldier:

> 'There were few in the regiment as healthy or as full of stamina as Hitler. With unbelievable toughness, he endured the greatest strains and never showed any weakness. The battle-ordinance, to which Hitler also belonged, was far more exposed to enemy fire than the companies themselves, for while the latter could always find cover in the terrain, the ordinance staff were constantly on the move with messages; and I am amazed even today, how Adolf Hitler came through the war so fortunately.'

Hitler was to become very familiar with the distant aspect of the town of Ypres. His war would start near the town and four years later it would also end there. Twenty four years later during one of his rambling monologues which were later collected together and published as 'Hitler's Table Talk', the *Fürher* recalled the first tantalising glimpse of the town which would remain within the grasp of the German armies but which would never fall to them.

> 'My first impression of Ypres was - towers, so near that I could all but touch them. But the little infantryman in his hole in the ground has a very small field of vision.'

Hitler's description of the battle for Gheluvelt is detailed at great length in his letter to Ernst Hepp. The fight clearly made a huge impression on him and he went to some trouble to ensure that Herr Hepp had all of the details. The situation was fluid and confused, and although trenches were beginning to appear on the battlefield, this was one of the last occasions on the Western Front on which armies would manouver in the open:

'Early, around 6 A.M., we came to an inn. We were with another company and it was not till 7 A.M. that we went out to join the dance. We followed the road into a wood, and then we came out in correct marching order on a large meadow. In front of us were guns in partially dug trenches and, behind these, we took up our positions in big hollows scooped out of the earth; and waited. Soon, the first lots of shrapnel came over, bursting in the woods, and smashing up the trees as though they were brushwood. We looked on interestedly, without any real idea of danger. No one was afraid. Every man waited impatiently for the command: "Forward!" The whole thing was getting hotter and hotter. We heard that some of us had been wounded. Five or six men brown as clay were being led along from the left, and we all broke into a cheer: six Englishmen with a machine gun! We shouted to our men marching proudly behind their prisoners. The rest of us just waited. We could scarcely see into the steaming, seething witches' caldron which lay in front of us. At last there came the ringing command: "Forward!"

We swarmed out of our positions and raced across the fields to a small farm. Shrapnel was bursting left and right of us, and the English bullets came whistling through the shrapnel; but we paid no attention to them. For ten minutes, we lay there; and then, once again, we were ordered to advance. I was right out in front, ahead of everyone in my platoon. Platoon-leader Stoever was hit. Good God! I had barely any time to think; the fighting was beginning in earnest! Because we were out in the open, we had to advance quickly. The captain was at the head. The first of our men had begun to fall. The English had set up machine guns. We threw ourselves down and crawled slowly along a ditch. From time to time someone was hit, we could not go on, and the whole company was stuck there. We had to lift the man out of the ditch. We kept on crawling until the ditch came to an end, and then we were out in the open field again. We ran fifteen or twenty yards, and then we found a big pool of water. One after another, we splashed through it, took cover, and caught our breath. But it was no place for lying low. We dashed out again at full speed into a forest that lay about a hundred yards ahead of us. There, after a while, we all found each other. But the forest was beginning to look terribly thin.

At this time there was only a second sergeant in command, a big tall splendid fellow called Schmidt. We crawled on our bellies to the edge of the forest, while the shells came whistling and whining above us; tearing tree trunks and branches to shreds. Then the shells came down again on the edge of the forest, flinging up clouds of earth, stones, and roots; and enveloping everything in a disgusting, sickening, yellowy-green vapor. We can't possibly lie here forever, we thought and, if we are going to be killed, it is better to die in the open. Then the Major came up. Once more we advanced. I jumped up and ran as fast as I could across meadows and beet fields, jumping over trenches, hedgerows, and barbed-wire entanglements; and then I heard someone shouting ahead of me: "In here! Everyone in here!" There was a long trench in front of me and, in an instant, I had jumped into it; and there were others in front of me, behind me, and left and right of me. Next to me were Württembergers, and under me were dead and wounded Englishmen.

The Württembergers had stormed the trench before us. Now I knew why I had landed so softly when I jumped in. About 250 yards to the left there were more English trenches; to the right the road to Leceloire was still in our possession. An unending storm of iron came screaming over our trench. At last, at ten o'clock, our artillery opened up in this sector. One - two - three - five - and so it went on. Time and again a shell burst in the English trenches in front of us. The poor devils came swarming out like ants from an ant heap, and we hurled ourselves at them. In a flash we had crossed the fields in front of us, and after bloody hand-to-hand fighting in some places, we threw (the enemy) out of one trench after another. Most of them raised their hands above their heads. Anyone who refused to surrender was mown down. In this way we cleared trench after trench.

At last we reached the main highway. To the right and left of us there was a small forest, and we drove right into it. We threw them all out of this forest, and then we reached the place where the forest came to an end and the open road continued. On the left lay several farms - all occupied - and there was withering fire. Right in front of us, men were falling. Our Major came up; quite fearless, and smoking calmly; with his adjutant, Lieutenant Piloty. The Major saw the situation at a glance, and ordered us to assemble, on both sides of the highway for an assault. We had lost our officers, and there were hardly any noncommissioned officers. So all of us, every one of us who was still walking, went running back to get reinforcements. When I returned the second time with a handful of stray Württembergers, the Major was lying on the ground with his chest torn open, and there was a heap of corpses all around him.

By this time, the only remaining officer was his adjutant. We were absolutely furious. "Herr Leutnant, lead us against them!" we all shouted. So we advanced straight into the forest, fanning out to the left, because there was no way of advancing along the road. Four times we went forward, and each time we were forced to retreat. From my company, only one other man was left besides myself, and then he, too, fell. A shot tore off the entire left sleeve of my tunic but, by a miracle, I remained unharmed. Finally, at 2 A.M. we advanced for the fifth time; and this time, we were able to occupy the farm and the edge of the forest. At 5 P.M., we assembled and dug in, a hundred yards from the road. So we went on fighting for three days in the same way, and on the third day the British were finally defeated. On the fourth evening we marched back to Werwick. Only then did we know how many men we had lost. In four days our regiment consisting of thirty-five hundred men was reduced to six hundred. In the entire regiment there remained only thirty officers. Four companies had to be disbanded. But we were all so proud of having defeated the British!'

Despite all the inherent evils of the job, Hitler had a love of soldiering which never left him, but even wearing his most rose-tinted glasses, he must have known that his audience was unlikely to be taken in by a description of eager units advancing towards each other singing patriotic songs. It is certainly true that in the intensive battles of the early war units would sing a snatch of *'Der Wacht Am Rhein'* which was the proscribed means of verbal recognition in the early stages of the war, but this activity had a distinct purpose. Hitler's less dramatic description of the withdrawal of the List Regiment from the line is much more convincing:

> *'After four days in the trenches we came back. Even our step was no longer what it had been. Boys of seventeen looked now like grown men. The rank and file of the List Regiment had not been properly trained in the art of warfare, but they knew how to die like old soldiers.'*

The official regimental history of the 16th RIR also described the fight around Gheluvelt in detail. It was a highly significant event in the history of the regiment and the fight for Gheluvelt on 31st October 1914 was described in suitably dramatic terms:

> *'The losses grow under the violent fire that the enemy hurls steel toward the attackers from cannons and machine-guns. They lean, and fall down on their knees among the hedges, mown down by a burst of fire; but the yawning gaps are always filled again by fresh fighters. Our artillery's lack of ammunition is clearly noticeable; it can offer the attack no effective support. Morning passes in tough, bloody stand-up fights. A horrifying battle fills the battlefield. The howls, hisses, crashes of the heavy shells of English naval cannons constantly bursting between the lines; the rolls of machine-gun salvos, and the clatter of infantry weapons; the fire rises from violent storms to raging assault, to eerie hurricane. Whole rows drop while pushing forward, crash back again, break in on themselves. Is it not mad to advance in this fire? And new waves push in, repeated hour after hour. The excitement is unproductive; all reserves are already used up. At last at 3 o'clock in the afternoon the enemy's key-point, the windmill - on the south-slope of the area from where so much (havoc) has been created - is brought under heavy fire by our artillery, is caught cleanly, and is shattered with a few direct hits. For a moment, enemy fire falls*

silent. It is like a deep, eerie breathing-space. Then it breaks out with
strengthening force: a single fire-spitting mouth of hell: but on - must
go on - forwards! Then, at the critical moment, the assault signal
of the buglers is heard over the whole fighting front! Knapsacks are
discarded; everyone pulls himself up: Bavarians, Saxons, Swabians,
all closed together; there are no more stops; only forwards! A thousand-
voiced "Hurrah" roars across the battlefield - a single violent victory
cry - and, like a wild surf, the storm waves throw themselves at the
village!--Gheluvelt is ours!'

Adolf Meyer of the List Regiment writing in his diary recalled one of the defining moments of the battle. This was the instant when Colonel List was killed by a British shell. It is not surprising that in all the confusion of battle there are differing accounts of the death of the Colonel. According to Meyer, List was killed fighting in the very front ranks. His diary entry records the effects of the fighting:

'Only a few regiments have had to give such a heavy toll in blood
in their first fight, the proud List Regiment had melted down to the
strength of a battalion, the brave regimental leader, Colonel List,
felled by a direct hit in the furthest forward line.'

Hans Mend writing in his book, gives a completely different account of the circumstances of the Colonel's death. Mend was an eye witness and recalled how he was on his way to see Colonel List, who was then engaged in setting up headquarters in the recently captured Gheluvelt chateaux. As he approached the building Mend witnessed what he described as a 'three heavy English shells' crashing into the building.' According to Mend this was the real cause of the death of Colonel List:

'I could see nothing any more, and could no longer breathe for
dust. Hearing cries of help coming from the chateaux, Mend rushed
forward and was able to describe the scene as an eyewitness in which
he attempted to assist in the rescue effort which was being performed
by a group of Saxons, a few telegraph operators sprang immediately to
the aid of the wounded. At once, one cried out: "The Bavarian colonel
is also dead!" In my horror, I left my horse unattended, and sprang to
the side of Colonel List, now covered by a tent flap. I lifted this away

and saw that blood welled from his mouth. Our brave commander,
who was a true leader of his troops, was no more.'

With the death of it's commander the regiment lost its immediate association with the name of it's first commander and was officially known from henceforth as the 16th Bavarian Reserve infantry Regiment (16th RIR), but the veterans such as Hitler continued to refer to the regiment by it's old title which is used interchangeably throughout the various personal accounts.

After four days of fierce fighting, the battle for Gheluvelt petered out with the Germans in control of the village. The prize had been won at great cost as Ignatz Westenkirchner recalled twenty years later when interviewed by Heinz A. Heinz:

'It was our baptism of fire. Four days we had of this at Becelaere
and Polygon Wood and Gheluvelt, four days and nights - sheer hell!
Of the three thousand men of the Regiment List, only five hundred
came safely out of it. The rest were killed, or wounded, or had
vanished. We had gone into battle as youngsters, we came out of it
worn, scarred, exhausted men. No longer recruits, we were soldiers
of the fighting line.'

This was the beginning of Hitler's war, and even he was soon forced to admit that a feeling of horror soon replaced the romantic fighting spirit. His description of the aftermath of the fighting is close to the reality of what had occured. The List Regiment had lost over two thirds of its strength in killed and wounded in those two brutal engagements.

'We went into rest billets for a couple of days at a place called
Werwick; then found ourselves in the thick of it again at Wytschaete.
We broke through the enemy line north of Messines and turned the left
flank of the trenches held by the London Scottish. But what ground or
advantage we gained at one moment was lost the next. The enemy was
forced to retire; but he came on again a few hours later.'

The List Regiment had paid a very heavy price in its first battle which can be attributed variously to a lack of training, inappropriate equipment and, most of all, a tendancy on the part of the German Officer Corps to underestimate and depreciate the fighting qualities of the British regulars who formed the opposition. This produced in the German rank and file a dangerous over-confidence which led to unnecessary risk taking and consequently to high casualties. As a result of the propaganda which they were fed, the men of the List Regiment were certain that they would prevail against an enemy which would simply melt away under their onslaught. The reality was completely different, their opposition were the regular units who were to become known to posterity as the famous Old Contemptables. These regular full time soldiers possessed a fierce determination to succeed, an aggressive attitude and had the training to make their presence felt in the field. The men of the Worcester Regiment and the Black Watch left an indelible impression on the mind of Adolf Hitler who later recalled his growing disillusionment in the pages of 'Mein Kampf':

'Faced with the Tommies in person in Flanders, after the very first days of battle the conviction dawned on each and every one of them that these Scotsmen did not exactly fit with the image they (the High Command) had fed us. The results were devastating for now the German soldier felt himself swindled by this propaganda.'

The victorious List Regiment withdrew, decimated and exhausted, to Commines to lick its wounds, as the men began to recover, the rumour mill was soon in action and the story began to circulate that the survivors were to be transferred to the Eastern Front. At the time of the Great War the Russian Front did not sound the note of dread which it would come to embody in the Second World War, and there was real appetite, even a wish, for the mooted transfer. The episode was reported in the official regimental history:

'In those days, although the regiment had no way of knowing, this wish was almost fulfilled. On 19th November an advance notice was sent to Crown Prince Rupprecht from the high command that six divisions, among them our 6th BRD, were to be placed under the command of Hindenburg, who had already won a decision in the East. But the List Regiment's luck would not be sweet. This did not happen.

Without rest, the difficult activity of fortification work began. New trenches were built, and connected by communications trenches... a *front was built with toughness and speed, by the sweat and blood of the best. This collaborative work was for Life; Death was the employer. The sooner it was complete, the less time for the enemy to fire, the deeper the trenches, the more secure the shelter, the safer the cover against shrapnel, the better to withstand shells. After establishing regimental headquarters in the Grand Palace at Messines, the List Regiment was to endure many harrowing weeks of constant pressure from British troops and artillery.'*

- CHAPTER 4 -

GEFREITER HITLER

FROM ALL OF THE EVIDENCE AVAILABLE TO us it would appear that the fighting for the farm at Becelaere and the village of Gheluvelt and was the only occasion on which Hitler fought with rifle in hand. By early November, the time of a brief action against the London Scottish near Wijtschaete, we know he was already serving as a regimental messenger. However the brief combat at Gheluvelt seems to have been enough for Hitler to distinguish himself in the field. It is conceivable that, even during his first taste of fighting near Gheluvelt, Hitler was already being entrusted to carry messages in the field. If that was the case it is not beyond the bounds of possibility that he may never have fired a shot in anger as a rifleman. Hans Mend certainly gives the impression that Hitler was already employed as a despatch runner at some time during the first engagement and describes Hitler in action: 'He lined up fearlessly for the most difficult messages, he was one of the best and most reliable battle ordinance men.' Mend also quoted the opinion of one of the officers of the List Regiment; 'I still can't understand how he puts his life at such risk when he owns not a single stone in Germany, he is certainly a strange one and lives in his own world, otherwise he is a capable individual.' Westenkirchner however gives a different account and clearly recalled Hitler fighting as an infantryman. We will never know the truth for certain but, in any event, Hitler certainly carried out the duties assigned to him to the satisfaction of his commander and in recognition for his service as a runner, by 9th November he was selected to serve permanently at Regimental headquarters. He was to achive the remarkable distinction of serving in that capacity and in that regiment for the next four years.

With the excitement of the opening engagements behind them, for the men of the List Regiment the misery of fighting in the Ypres salient soon took hold. Hans Mend wrote an evocative passage in his memoirs which summed up the drudgery of those days as the reality of the true nature of this war to end all wars began to make itself known.

> 'Days and weeks passed, for all of us in a state of the greatest stress, which cost many good comrades their lives.... Even if filthy, sulfur-yellow like a canary, with bullet holes in the great coat or dispatch case, the lucky ones among us were glad to be able to march safely back into our quarters. With steaming coffee or a "Blue Henry"[7] (a Schnapps) the adventures of the preceding day were made light of, through wit and humor. In all of this, Adolf Hitler was no spoilsport, on the contrary, he livened things up with his ideas and interruptions: but he never spoke about his work.'

Hitler may not have spoken about his work to Mend, but he did send a very lengthy letter in February 1915 to Ernst Hepp which contains a great deal of detail concerning Hitler's early service in the war and touches upon the award of the Iron Cross Second Class:

> 'Since that time we have been continually in the front lines. I was proposed for the Iron Cross, the first time in Messines, then again at Wytschaete by Lieutenant Colonel Engelhardt, who was our regimental commander. Four other soldiers were proposed for the Iron Cross at the same time. Finally, on 2nd December, I received the medal.
>
> My job now is to carry dispatches for the staff. As for the mud, things are a bit better here, but also more dangerous. In Wytschaete during the first day of the attack three of us eight dispatch riders were killed, and one was badly wounded. The four survivors and the man who was wounded were cited for their distinguished conduct. While they were deciding which of us should be awarded the Iron Cross, four company commanders came to the dugout. That meant that the four of us had to step out. We were standing some distance away about five minutes later when a shell slammed into the dugout, wounding

---

7. This was the soldier's term for a schnapps in the German Army.

Lieutenant Colonel Engelhardt and killing or wounding the rest of his staff. This was the most terrible moment of my life. We worshipped Lieutenant Colonel Engelhardt.

I am sorry, I will have to close now. The really important thing for me is to keep thinking about Germany. From eight in the morning to five in the afternoon, day after day, we are under heavy artillery fire. In time even the strongest nerves are shattered by it. I keep thinking about Munich, and there is not one man here who isn't hoping that we shall soon finish off this rabble once and for all, make mincemeat of them, at whatever the cost. The hope is that those of us who have the good fortune to see our homeland again will find it purer and less corrupted by foreign influence. The sacrifices and misery exacted daily from hundreds of thousands of people, the rivers of blood flowing every day against an international world of enemies will, we hope, result in smashing Germany's external enemies and bring about the destruction of our internal internationalism. That would be better than any territorial gains. As for Austria, it will come about as I have already told you.

Once more I express my heartiest gratitude and remain your devoted and grateful ADOLF HITLER.'

The same Lieutenant Colonel Engelhardt whom Hitler mentions in his letter obviously harboured a measure of mutual respect for Hitler. In a 1932 pamphlet, 'Facts and Lies', he is quoted describing Hitler's act of bravery which it is thought led to the award of the Iron Cross 2nd Class.

'Once as I emerged from the wood at Wytschaete during a fierce attack, in order to make some observations, Hitler and an orderly from the Regimental Staff, planted themselves bang in front of me to shield me with their own bodies from machine-gun fire.' [8]

The fact that Hitler had distinguished himself in the fighting was also recognised by him being awarded *gefreiter* status. In the English speaking world the term *gefreiter* is problematic and has caused some difficulties

---

8. Englehardt is quoted in the pamphlet entitled *'Tatsachen und Lügen um Hitler'* (Facts and Lies About Adolf Hitler) published in 1932 in Munich.

in interpreting the Hitler story. The Imperial German Army used a large number of terms to indicate the status of a soldier which had no direct counterpart in the English or American forces. Hitler for example could be referred to by the title *kreigsfreiwilliger*, or wartime volunteer, which was used to differentiate professional career soldiers from those who had joined for the duration. Over the centuries the German military tradition has also harnessed a variety of unique incentives to encourage good conduct in the ranks. One of these was to recognise reliable private soldiers (who were known by the title *infanterist* in the Bavarian army) and rewarding them with an easier life. The word *gefrieter* evolved from older German and Dutch – meaning 'freed' or 'liberated' person. The award of the title *gefreiter* brought with it a series of negative rights which meant the the *gefreitene* did not have to perform many of the most menial duties which the private soldiers loathed so much. The holder of the title *gefreiter* was literally freed from sentry duty. It is important to realise that *gefreiter* was not a rank which brought with it the right to issue orders to other men, as such it was little more a signifier which indicated that this man was considered to be a trustworthy private soldier. A better term might be Private First Class, but the revised status also brought with it a tiny rise in pay, an *infanterist* received 70 pfennigs per day while a *gefreiter* received 75 pfennigs.[9]

Hitler was elevated to *gefreiter* status in November 1914, but in contrast to the popular conception in the UK and the USA, he was certainly not promoted to the equivalent rank of a corporal. In the Bavarian army of 1914 the rank of corporal had its own directly equivalent rank which was called *korporal*. In the Prussian army the equivalent term was *unteroffizier*. It is clearly a substantial error therefore to translate *gefreiter* to corporal, but regrettably this is what so often happens. In the Bavarian army of 1914 *korporal* was the lowest rank from which orders could be given to subordinates. The *'gefreitene'* on the other hand, although they were recognised as reliable private soldiers, had no power of command over other men. The term helped to

---

9. Source the 1918 'German Army Handbook'.

differentiate between proven and unproven *infanterists*, it aided Officers and NCOs to identify those who had distinguished themselves and who could be counted upon. To assist that process such men were addressed as 'liberated' or *'gefreitene'*. The holder of the title remained an ordinary private soldier nonetheless and was not authorised to give any form of command. It certainly is confusing but the reality is that Hitler had merely been recognised as a reliable and trustworthy soldier and was rewarded by being exempted from sentry duties.

Hitler's contemporaries such as Westenkirchner understood the sub-text of the situation and in the inter-war translations of Nazi books such as Heinz's 'Germany's Hitler', Hitler is referred to as a private and later as a lance corporal. Alexander Moritz Frey however consistently refers to Hitler as a 'private' and indeed this appears in the title of the unpublished article, which came to light after the war, 'The Unknown Private - Personal Memories of Hitler'.

In order to get round this difficulty the term *gefreiter* is frequently equated with the British rank of lance-corporal, but even this is not altogether helpful as there was no direct equivalent in the Bavarian army. The mistaken assumption that a 1914 Bavarian *gefrieter* was equivalent to an non-commissioned officer took root during World War II. To add to the confusuion, by 1940 the role of the *gefreiter* in the Wehrmacht had changed to a role which was indeed equiavalent to a junior non-commissioned officer such as a lance corporal. The upshot of this difficulty in translation has led to the creation of the popular myth that Hitler was promoted with the equivalent rank of *unteroffizier* or *korporal*, this is simply untrue. Of one thing we can be certain; Hitler never was a corporal.

After the brief flurry of excitement which surrounded their arrival in Flanders, the men of the List Regiment soon had to settle down to the routine of life in the waterlogged and muddy trenches which were to become infamous during the Battle of Paschendale. Hans Mend summed up the miserable experience of the first year in the trenches.

'It was of small satisfaction to us that the positions of our opponents
were just as bad as our own, for the English had also suffered heavily

from the mass of water forcing its way into the trenches. Once they tried, by opening the sluice valves, to flood our position but our pioneers had prevented this plan in time…. To put it bluntly, the way our troops existed was not to be envied.'

Despite all of the privations, Hitler certainly demonstrated a keen appetite for soldiering, but Hans Mend noted the gloomy mien which Gefreiter Hitler had begun to exhibit. Mend writing about this period recalled how one day he observed an infantryman standing with his rifle at his feet lost in contemplation:

'From his stance, I immediately recognized Adolf Hitler. Two dead men, in whom he seemed very interested, lay in front of him. He looked around and stretched his head, as though sensing danger. But in spite of the greatest danger to life and limb, he remained next to the dead men. Once he turned in my direction, probably since he recognized me and wanted to see how I would get through this crater field. Next day I asked what he found so interesting and Hitler answered, "I took a look at two dead men on whom grass was already growing." I replied that it was absolutely unnecessary to remain at that place, unless you want to catch moles. Hitler tugged at his mustache, as if to say, "Dispatch rider Mend, you look after yourself, I'll look after myself." Before we parted, I remarked: "Your bones could be lying in that corner of the battlefield at Messines."

Ignatz Westenkirchner also recalled this settling down period in the wretched landscape around Ypres. In his 1934 interview with Heinz A. Heinz he described the course of the first winter:

'The weather got ever colder and colder. As the winter set in, the line hereabouts established itself and the fighting was no longer so fierce until the turn of the year. When I say this I mean it wasn't so fierce in comparison with what was to come later! Looking back now, all that business at Becelaere and Wytschaete was child's play to the fighting still ahead. For the most part all that first winter we occupied trenches between Messines and Wulverghem. Our line was consolidated by then and it held like steel for four years. By now Hitler was a trench runner, whose duty was to keep up communication

*between Company and Regimental Headquarters. There were eight or
ten of us altogether. We were very pally and made a mob by ourselves.
There were even times when things couldn't be said to be too bad -
when we got parcels from home and letters. We shared out, of course.
Sometimes, even, we had a game with 'Tommy.' We stuck a helmet
on the point of a bayonet and shoved it above the parapet, when it
would be sure to draw immediate fire. Even Hitler, who was usually
so serious, saw the fun of this. He used to double himself up with
laughter.'*

Hitler later maintained that his enthusiasm for the war cooled down
gradually, but the realisation for most of his comrades was harsh and
sudden. Any remaining and exuberant spirits were soon quelled by the
fear of ever-present death. Self preservation inevitably took over from
military ardour and even a gung-ho character like Hitler recognised this
moment when duty was eclipsed by survival:

*'A time came when there arose within each one of us a conflict
between the urge to self-preservation and the call of duty. And I had
to go through that conflict too. As Death sought its prey everywhere
and unrelentingly a nameless Something rebelled within the weak
body and tried to introduce itself under the name of Common Sense;
but in reality it was Fear, which had taken on this cloak in order to
impose itself on the individual.'*

The cooling of martial ardour wasn't just limited to the German
side of the line. On 25th December 1914 the famous Christmas truce
took place and was most marked just to the south of Messines; almost
exactly where Hitler's regiment was stationed. Heinz A Heinz writing
in 'Germany's Hitler', gives us the view from the English side of the
trenches and quotes Field-Marshal French:

*'It was that first winter of the War, the Germans took a very bold
initiative at several points along our Front in trying to establish some
form of fraternisation. It began by individual unarmed men running
from the German trenches across to ours holding Xmas trees above
their heads. These overtures were in some places favourably received
and fraternisation of a limited kind took place during the day. It*

appeared that a little feasting went on, and junior officers, non-coms, and men on either side conversed together in No Man's Land. When this was reported to me I issued immediate orders to prevent any recurrence of such conduct....'

According to Heinz, popular opinion in England was against the belligerent attitude of the Generals. Heinz fondly imagined, and not without some good reason, that the sentimental English public liked the idea of a Christmas truce, and credited the Christian gesture, to the 'gentler Bavarians' in the Imperial German Army. In any event the truce was short lived and was never to be repeated.

The List Regiment was soon plunged back into the unremitting grind of daily life at the front. The course of the Great War was inexorably turning against Germany and allied superiority in men and material was already beginning to make itself felt. In March 1915 there was an unexpected new posting for the regiment. The British had regained the initiative and were ready to unleash a major offensive which would become known to posterity as the Battle of Neuve Chapelle. Balthasar Brandmayer was another of Hitler's comrades who wrote a memoir of his war-time service alongside Hitler. He had not seen action in the opening battles of 1914 but he was with the List Regiment as it was rushed in to position to defend Neuve Chapelle:

'Alarms were sounded at noon from all directions.... An hour later we found ourselves sitting in a military train, where this would take us no one knows. Some suspect that we will be going to Russia, others to Lorraine. The overloaded train rolls slowly and carefully into the deepening night. We freeze: scarcely a word is spoken.'

The sudden train journey was far shorter than expected and those who had hopes of a transfer to Russia were again disappointed. The men de-trained and once more found themselves in Lille, and learned of the disconcerting news that British regiments had broken through the German front line, as each of the companies of the List Regiment arrived they were formed into ranks and marched off as quickly as possible to a new destination; the town of Neuve Chapelle. The British had succeeded in making a small incursion into the German lines and the fighting was tough and bloody. In order to recapture the lost territory the 6th BRD, Hitler's parent division, was thrown into battle in piecemeal fashion. Regiments, battalions, detachments, companies, and batteries were rushed onto the battlefield as soon as they arrived at the railway station, and as a result were divided up among the Prussian formations holding the line. According to the Bavarian official History the result was a motley crew which was only just able to stitch together a defence. Hans Mend was an eye witness to the events and he recalled the confusion bordering on panic as the German's scrambled to react to the British offensive:

'The confusion came into being because the different formations from our regiment, as they disembarked from their trains, were immediately marched to the Front and had gone into action, on their own account, between Prussian troops. The battle orderlies, Hitler, Lippert, Schmidt, and Weiss had the task, in so far as possible, to re-establish the connection, which was made all the more difficult by the frightful fire and the soggy ground underfoot. Hitler said later in Fournes that he had to deliver reports by creeping forward from one shell-hole to another, and that sometimes the sulfur fumes only allowed him to see 10 metres to the Front. During the lulls in the fighting he paced around like a restless tiger in the farm at Halpegarde.... Even the Colonel said: "I can scarcely believe that my orderlies can come through this fire..." The most dangerous time for a dispatch runner is delivering a message for the first time from a new position. I said to Hitler "You're a mole. You'll come through all right, just don't let them shoot you in the guts." "That's my business, my dear Mend," Hitler replied that the communications trenches leading to the positions further forward provided little protection, they were not deep enough and already, on the first crossings, caused many casualties. Adolf Hitler had to take these dangerous paths several times daily and, if he wanted to come through safe and sound, was obliged to crawl rather than march. Not even the slightest movement escaped English snipers, exposed to the heavy barrage on the way from Fromelles to the fighting zone.... Hitler reported "Every shell-hole

is being bitterly contested. Because of our barrage, the English have been cut off from all possible help. Many are hanging on the electric barbed-wire, and screaming horribly." As we knew him to be a man who never exaggerated and, who expressed himself carefully in such situations, we knew now that a bloody fight was being waged. His expression also attracted attention. He must have seen much horror and have joined in the fighting himself; the expression of the eyes in his thin yellow face told us much.'

For most men in the trenches the lure of self preservation outweighed the desire to serve one's country; Hitler was different, for him the call of duty took precedence over self preservation. At Neuve Chapelle, the amazing reservoir of will power which Hitler was able to summon up on occasion, asserted its incontestable mastery. His sense of duty, obedience to the national cause and an obsessive devotion to the German Reich had won out and Hitler remained steadfastly obedient to his adopted country's call even in this most unforgiving of environments. At a more mundane level Hitler was also noticeably different from the other men in his unit, as he had no contact with his family in the shape of his sister Paula, or his half sister Angela, and he received no parcels from home. This was noted by his colleagues such as Ignatz Westenkirchner:

'He owned up to me sometimes how stoney broke he was. Poor chap, he never had a cent! I blurted it right out once – "Haven't you got anyone back home? Isn't there anyone to send you things?" "No," he answered, "at least, no one but a sister, and goodness only knows where she is by this time." There were letters and parcels awaiting us there - all except for Hitler. He just looked the other way and busied himself knocking the mud off his boots and doing what he could to clean his shirt.'

Hans Mend was another of the men of the List Regiment who also noted the sad situation of Gefreiter Hitler who received little in the way of mail and no parcels whatsoever:

'When he was not fired at, he would often say on his return: "Today an old woman would have had no trouble in getting through"…. Hitler often looked completely exhausted; the best nerves can fail.

However, he always pulled himself together.... I never saw him receive a field packet. Nor would he accept presents from us, though we often made the offer. Occasionally he refused with a brief thank you. He was uninterested in home leave. The trenches and Fromelles were his world and what lay beyond did not exist for him.'

As Mend observed, by early 1915 Hitler had thrown himself fully into the world of soldiering. The List Regiment was his new family and he proved himself a dedicated and genuinely courageous soldier. All of the main witnesses to Hitler's deeds in the trenches are united in testifying to the fact that he was absolutely dedicated to his duty and did not shirk from even the toughest and most dangerous assignments. However, that is not to say that Hitler was popular. He certainly was not an easy companion. Some of his colleagues recall that he was a tiresome individual who marched to the beat of a different drummer, his main critic in this respect is Alexander Moritz Frey.

Moritz Frey was serving in the ranks of the List regiment alongside Hitler, he was a writer turned medic. After the war Frey became a very popular German science fiction writer who reached his peak of popularity in the thirties, he also contributed to the long running Bavarian based humour magazine *Simplissimus*. Long after his death in 1954, an obscure unpublished essay by Frey entitled 'The Unknown Private - Personal Memories of Hitler', was discovered in an archive in the German town of Marbach. Frey was no friend of Hitler's and unwaveringly refused to join the Nazi party. He remained critical of Hitler even into the thirties and he eventually had to flee the country when the attentions of the SA grew too strong. It was during the war that Moritz Frey first became sceptical of Hitler. He mistrusted him and soon formed the view that the thin Austrian was a schemer and conniver who used his talents with words to his own ends, but even Frey had to testify to the fact that Hitler was not a coward and, although he was no hero, he did not lack the courage to be able to withstand the rigours of the front:

'When people claim that he had been a coward, that's not true. But he also wasn't brave, he lacked the composure for that. He was

always alert, ready to act, back-stabbing, very concerned about himself. All his comradeship was an act - an act cleverly chosen for the simple and naïve - to make himself popular and to create a striking impression. He knew the tricks that one could use to throw nuggets to the youngsters that they would happily swallow.'

Not everyone who fought alongside Hitler was in accord with Moritz Frey's harsh views. A young Lieutenant called Fritz Wiedemann respected Hitler's qualities as a soldier despite his decidedly 'unmilitary' bearing. Wiedemann would later be promoted to Captain and was destined to become Hitler's adjutant from 1935 until 1939, when he was dismissed following a disagreement over Hitler's foreign policy. Despite his differences with Hitler, Wiedemann was firmly of the opinion that Hitler was a fine soldier and that Hitler's account of his war experiences in *'Mein Kampf'* was essentially true. Wiedmann eventually fled to America, but he too was adamant that Hitler fundamentally told the truth concerning his war record. 'I never caught him lying or exaggerating when he told of his recollections'.

Balthasar Brandmayer was another comrade from the Great War who produced a written account of his service alongside Hitler. He was not present during the opening battles and first met Adolf Hitler on 30th May 1915 after recovering from injuries during the 9th May attack on Neuve Chapelle. Brandmayer returned to the ranks of the 16th RIR and was given the position of *meldegänger* and joined Hitler's tight knit little group. Writing in his memoirs Brandmayer later recounted his first encounter with Hitler in a bunker occupied by the Regimental runners:

'He had only come back fatigued after a delivery. I looked at him for the first time in my life. We stood eye to eye facing one another.... He was like a skeleton, his face pale and colorless. Two piercingly dark eyes, which struck me especially, stared out of deep sockets. His prominent mustache was unkempt. Forehead and facial expression suggested high intelligence. I can still see him today as he stood before me then, loosening his belt buckle. Along with Max Mund, Adolf Hitler became my inseparable comrade.'

Unlike the rest of the grumblers and moaners who make up armies everywhere, Hitler, it seems, was obsessive in his dedication to duty. We are told he was a ready volunteer for difficult missions and always seemed to find a way to get the message through the most threatening shell fire even if he was sometimes reduced to crawling on his belly like a snake. Private Westenkirchner was another of the List regiment who felt that Hitler was unfairly maligned after the Great War. He gave vent to his frustrations when interviewed by Heinz A. Heinz in 1934 and, as a Nazi supporter, Heinz was naturally quick to take up the argument on his *Fürher's* part.

> *'Among the innumerable libels with which the Führer has no time to concern himself, if he is to get on with the job of governing Germany at all, is that which accuses him of skulking during the War. He is supposed to have managed somehow or other to have kept well out of the firing line.'*

By 1932 the 'innumerable libels' which Heinz referred to were increasingly appearing in print and Germany's left leaning newspapers were quick to seize upon any opportunity to criticise Hitler. In order to refute the allegations a number of pamphlets concerning Hitler and his service in the Great War were prepared and issued to the public. The first was written by Dagobert Dürr and was entitled *'Adolf Hitler, der deutsche Arbeiter und Frontsoldat'* (Adolf Hitler the German worker and front-line soldier). It was published during the first round of the 1932 presidential election. Heinz A. Heinz was able to draw upon this and the later 1932 pamphlet entitled *'Tatsachen und Lügen um Hitler'* (Facts and Lies About Adolf Hitler)[10] to support his case that Hitler was a trusted and doughty fighter. The Nazi pamphlets were both published in the wake of the 1932 court case which Hitler successfully pursued against *Echo Der Woche* which had published an article which was critical of Hitler's Great War service. That court case was part of the fall out which marked the bitterly fought 1932 presidential campaign,

---

10. A full transcript of the pamphlet can be found at http://www.calvin.edu/academic/cas/gpa/tatsachenundluegen.htm.

the second round of which was held on 10th April 1932. According to the 'Facts and Lies' pamphlet Hitler also took action against a member of the S.P.D. who had falsely claimed that Hitler had received a prison sentence for deserting the German army, and for which he had been granted amnesty from Kurt Eisner. The allegation was adjudged to be slanderous and in this instance the defendant had to pay a 50 Mark fine. The S.P.D. party was also the principal publisher of the story that Hitler had shirked his Great War duties. At Fournes in particular, it was alleged that Hitler had always been 'far from the action.' The court was unimpressed from the outset and a temporary ban was imposed on an S.P.D. pamphlet. In the subsequent court proceedings, the judge heard all of the evidence including the testimony of many of Hitler's former comrades. On the basis of the evidence before him he ruled that the claim was patently untrue. We should not overlook the fact that his judgement was based on an impressive number of sworn statements by witnesses, either on paper or directly before the court.

The 'Facts and Lies' pamphlet published on behalf of the Nazi party in 1932 is particularly interesting as it reproduces the testimony of a substantial array of accurate official statements which were used in the trial. However, the pamphlet has been dismissed by some authorities, Thomas Weber in particular, disregards the court testimony as being the inevitable product of the bond between former comrades, but there is no evidence to support the suggestion that Hitler's former comrades went out of their way to lie on his behalf. The pamphlet should therefore be taken at face value and it goes a long way towards producing the hard evidence which contradicts the idea that Hitler was a coward who skulked in the rear areas. No less than three of Gefreiter Hitler's commanding officers gave evidence in the trial with the highest appreciation of his soldierly qualities. These men adhered to a strict code of honour and held the utmost respect for the organs of the state. Their evidence certainly stood up well in a court of law in what we must remember was still the pre-Nazi era. There is therefore no justifiable reason why these statements should not carry proper weight in the historical record. The 'Facts and Lies' pamphlet was quick to capitalise on the court victory over the S.P.D and its newspaper, and in order to make further capital the Nazis reproduced a number of excerpts from the sworn statements:

'… I want to stress that, when during the attack on the axe-shaped piece of forest (later called the Bavarian Forest), I left the cover of the forest near Wytschaete to better observe the attack, Hitler and another courier from the regimental staff, the volunteer Bachmann, placed themselves in front of me to protect me from machine gun fire with their own bodies.'

Signed: Engelhardt, Major General (retired),
former commander of the Bavarian R.-R.-F.-R. 16 (List).

'… I can only give former Corporal Hitler the greatest praise for his extraordinary accomplishments. Fournes was a village behind the regiment's battle line. It served as a recovery area for battalion relieved from the front, and also served as the seat of the regimental staff during calmer periods. The village was within the danger zone, and was frequently under rather heavy fire. During battle, the regimental headquarters was moved about 3/4 of an hour forward to Fournelles, and orders had to be carried to the front line. The path was often under enemy machine gun and artillery fire. I can never remember a single time when Hitler was absent from his post. Hitler may wear the medals he earned with pride…'

Signed: Satny, Colonel (retired),
former commander of the Bavarian R.-F.-R. 16 (List).

'Mr. Hitler, as corporal, was a courier for the regimental staff, and was not only always willing to carry out hard tasks, but did so with distinction. I stress that the List Regiment, as might be expected from its history, was at the toughest parts of the front, fighting in frequent major battles…'

Signed: Baligand, Colonel (retired),
last commander of the Bavarian R.-F.-R. 16 (List).

'... At particularly dangerous points I often was asked for volunteers, and at such times Hitler regularly volunteered, and without hesitation...'

Signed: Bruno Horn,
Lieutenant with the Bavarian R.-F.-R. 16 (List).

'... Hitler never hesitated in the least in carrying out even the most difficult order, and very often took on the most dangerous duties for his comrades.

Couriers for the regimental staff had to be among the most reliable people, because serving as a regimental courier during battles and skirmishes required iron nerves and a cool head. Hitler always did his duty, and even after his severe thigh wound, volunteered to be sent back to his regiment from the reserve battalion immediately after his release from the hospital...'

Signed: Max Amann,
former sergeant with the Bavarian R.-F.-R. 16 (List).

'... I often met Corporal Adolf Hitler as he served as courier to and from the front. Anyone who understands the duties of a courier - and any soldier who has served at the front does - knows what it means, day after day and night after night to move through artillery fire and machine gun fire from the rear...'

Signed: Joseph Lohr,
officer candidate with the Bavarian R.-F.-R. 16 (List).

'... It is true that Hitler was nearly blinded by a courier mission during a heavy gas attack, even though he was wearing a gas mask...'

Signed: Jakob Weiß,
NCO with the Bavarian R.-F.-R. 16 (List).

'... Hitler received the Iron Cross, First Class, during the spring or summer of 1918 for his outstanding service as a courier during the great offensive of 1918, and in particular for his personal capture of

a French officer and about 15 men, whom he suddenly encountered during a mission, and as a result of his quick thinking and decisive action, captured.

Hitler was seen by his fellow couriers, and many others in the regiment, as one of the best and bravest soldiers.'

Signed: Ernst Schmidt,
with the Bavarian R.-F.-R. 16 (List) from November 1914 until
October 1918.

According to the pamphlet, the most sensational moment of the trial came during the testimony of Hitler's regimental comrade Michel Schlehuber. Schlehuber was a Social Democrat and had been a trade union member for 35 years. He was certainly not a Nazi and was actually called as a witness by the opposing side; it was to prove a disastrous decision for Hitler's opponents:

'I have known Hitler since the departure for the front of the Bavarian R.-I-R. 16. I came to know Hitler as a good soldier and faultless comrade. I never saw Hitler attempt to avoid any duty or danger. I was part of the division from first to last, and never heard anything then or afterwards bad about Hitler. I was astonished when I later read unfavorable things about Hitler's service as a soldier in the newspapers. I disagree entirely with Hitler on political matters, and give this testimony only because I highly respect Hitler as a war comrade.'

Signed: Michael Schlehuber

The overwhelming testimonies given by Hitler's former colleagues appear to be genuine. They were certainly strong enough to convince the court and stood up to the rigours of the German legal system at a time before Hitler had tasted political power. There is no question of any legal fix and we must surely therefore accept the verdict of the court.

It is clear from the weight of support that Hitler was certainly not, as he is all too frequently depicted, the lonely outcast devoid of friends

On 29th May 1913 a police report form for Adolf Hitler was created by the Munich police. Although Hitler had already arrived in Munich on 25th May 1913, an arrival date of 26th May 1913 was stated. From the document it is clear that he intended to stay for two years.

The police report form for Rudolf Häusler proves that he and Hitler came to Munich on 25th May 1913, and that the two lived together in a small room at the tailor Joseph Popp's house from 25th May 1913 to 16th February 1914.

A certificate of residence from the 10th September 1929, and a notification card to prove that Hitler came to Munich in May 1913 and not 1912, as Hitler stated time and again.

Although Hitler stated that he neither received nor requested money from relatives, the district court noted that on the 4th May 1911 Adolf Hitler received large amounts from his aunt Johanna Polzl, to cover his studies as a painter.

A watercolour painted by Adolf Hitler, from the collection of Heinrich Hoffmann. In the years of 1913 and 1914, Hitler often painted this view of the oldest house in Munich. The building would survive the war and this very scene may be viewed today.

During the years of the Third Reich, the Popp's house at No. 34 Schleißheimerstraße, carried a plaque indicating that Hitler had lived there until August 1914. Hitler had indeed lived here with Rudolf Häusler from 25th May 1913 to 16th February 1914. Hitler remained here as a sole lodger until 16th August 1914 when he left for active service with the Imperial German Army.

A Bavarian officer reading out the German declaration of war in August 1914.

On Sunday, 2nd August 1914, a twenty-five year old Adolf Hitler was amongst thousands of people gathered at the Odeonsplatz in Munich. The crowd joined in exuberant enthusiasm for the war and Heinrich Hoffman was on hand to record the scene. He later identified Hitler as a figure in the crowd.

The earliest known photograph of Regimentsordonnanzen (Regimental Orderlies) and messengers Ernst Schmidt, Anton Bachmann and Adolf Hitler. Seated at Hitler's feet is the English Terrier named Foxl, who came to be Hitler's most treasured companion. The photograph was taken in April 1915 in Fournes.

Hitler with his comrades in September 1915, at the Regimental Command Post in Fromelles. Photograph by Hans Bauer: (Front row, left to right) Adolf Hitler, Josef Wurm, Karl Lippert, Josef Kreidmayer. (Middle row, left to right) Karl Lanzhammer, Ernst Schmidt, Jacob Höfele, Jacob Weiss. (Back row) Karl Tiefenböck.

In this photograph taken at the beginning of September 1916, Hitler is seen alongside his colleagues and his faithful dog Foxl in the rear area at Fournes. (Front row, left to right) Adolf Hitler, Balthasar Brandmayer, Anton Bachmann, Max Mund. (Back row, left to right) Ernst Schmidt, Johann Sperl, Jacob Weiss and Karl Tiefenböck.

The badly damaged town of Fromelles, where the Regimental Headquarters of the 16th RIR was situated from 17th March 1915 to 27th September 1916. Even in the rear areas, such as this, long-range shelling was a constant menace.

Orderly Sergeant Max Amann (left) pictured at La Bassée station in March 1917.

A German position at Fromelles, pre-1915. Trenches such as these were frequently knee-deep in water.

The conditions in the water-logged frontline trenches near Fromelles were appalling, as this photograph from May 1915 graphically demonstrates. The men of the 16th RIR lived and fought in these conditions.

German trenches on the Aisne during the Great War. The photograph is undated, but the men are not wearing helmets so this is early in the war, possibly 1914 or early 1915.

Adolf Hitler in 1916 in the rear area at Fournes.

Adolf Hitler and Karl Lippert in mid-1915 in Fournes.

Adolf Hitler, then a battalion-messenger, seen in May 1915 with his rifle slung over his shoulder. Hitler was in the process of delivering a message. This photograph first appeared in the Official Regimental History of the 16ᵗʰ RIR.

Hitler, accompanied by Max Amann and Ernst Schmidt and aides, after the victory over France on 26th May 1940. The group were photographed on their tour to visit the positions they had occupied during Great War in Flanders.

Hitler with his comrades in May 1916 in Fournes: Balthasar Brandmayer (front), (left to right seated) Johann Wimmer, Josef Inkofer, Karl Lanzhammer, Adolf Hitler, (left to right standing) Johann Sperl, Max Mund.

Hitler with (right to left) Max Amann, Wehrmacht adjutant Gerhard Engel, Ernst Schmidt and adjutant Julius Schaub on 26th April 1940 at the same location in Fournes, some 24 years later.

Hitler (left with helmet), and next to him Balthasar Brandmayer, pose for the camera in a bunker near the frontline section of Reincourt-Villers in September 1916.

Hitler on 26th October 1916, in the Prussian Association of the Red Cross hospital in Beelitz near Berlin, where he was brought after being wounded on 5th October 1916.

From soldier to Führer.
These four portraits illustrate the change in Hitler's face and moustache between the years of 1915 to 1921.
(Clockwise from top left) Hitler pictured in 1915, 1916, 1919 and 1921.

A photograph of members of the POW camp guard contingent at Traunstein taken in early January 1919. Hitler (left circle) and Ernst Schmidt (right circle) served here guarding Russian POWs until 11th February 1919.

From 20th February to 8th March 1919, Hitler (seen standing in the centre at the rear of the photograph) helped to guard the Munich Central Train Station, he is pictured here with his fellow guards.

The remains of the German trenches at Wytschaete near Ypres. Hitler served on this sector of the front and was awarded the Iron Cross 2nd Class for his actions at almost this exact spot.

The remains of a German block house at the Bayernwald near Ypres. Hitler spent the war carrying messages to and from locations such as this.

and lacking in respect from his comrades. That is not to say that Hitler behaved in a regular manner. He was not typical of the average soldier and Hans Mend again noticed his changes of mood, which he felt may have been connected to Hitler's increasingly poor health:

'In twenty-three months had not once spent half a day in Lille, had never taken home leave and never once reported sick was suddenly very sick and coughed heavily, but none of us could convince him to report to the doctor.'

Mend blamed the unhealthy conditions at the front for Hitler's declining health and noted that although there was little snow or frost, the area was subject to persistent falls of freezing rain. It heralded a miserable Christmas and Mend noted that during the second Christmas of the war the sickly Hitler was apparently even more miserable than his long suffering comrades.

'Many lay in wet clothes, with a high fever, on wet bunks in the barracks. Only a few were able to dry their uniforms in the ovens installed there; most, therefore, returned on the march to the Front with the same wet covering they'd arrived in. Clinging to the body and soaked through with mud and dirt, these bits of uniform offered no protection at all against the cold. Mass illness was the inevitable consequence, and whole companies had to be placed on sick leave by the doctor. The only advantage our troops had during the wet season was that they had no fear of attack by the enemy, for they were just as badly off. When Hitler came back from the trenches at night, he often lay on his wooden bunk in wet clothes. During the three days of Christmas, he spoke not a word to anyone, and we were unable to explain why he was so surly. At that time, he was perhaps taking it to heart that everyone at home had forgotten him, and that nobody had sent either a Christmas greeting or present.... When he returned from a mission on Christmas Day, he sat deep in thought, sunk in a corner with his helmet still on his head, and no one was capable of stirring him out of his apathy.'

In marked contrast to Hans Mend, who was sympathetic to Hitler's plight, Alexander Moritz Frey maintained a very circumspect view of

Hitler. He suspected him of playing to the gallery and attempting to create a false picture of dedication and suffering. In contrast to Mend's claim that Hitler never reported sick, Moritz Frey recalled how Hitler had refused some routine medication which Moritz Frey had prescribed for a throat infection. Moritz Frey formed the opinion that Hitler did this in order that he could play the martyr's role and gain additional recognition for his selflessness:

> 'I gave him some sort of tablet to swallow. He had a mild temperature and a raw red throat. Although it was as good as nothing and it would normally have been ignored at the front, I advised him nonetheless to register for a doctor's appointment the next day. He thought for a moment, hesitated -- and then shook his head... clenched determination in his eyes. No, he didn't want that, he said opaquely. In the later course of his illness, he made sure that it was talked about among his fellow soldiers and that it also came to the ears of the officers that Hitler has a 'terrific throat infection' but is doing his duty nonetheless.'

Given the ineffectual qualities of many medicines dispensed at the time, this may appear to be a rather harsh judgement but Moritz Frey was a man of conviction and he remained a genuine opponent of Hitler. Almost alone among the old soldiers of the 16th RIR Regiment, Moritz Frey refused to surrender to the allure of the Nazi party even though Hitler later extended a personal invitation for him to join.

- CHAPTER 5 -

ENTER FOXL

ALTHOUGH MANY OF HIS COMRADES appear to have held a high regard for Adolf Hitler, in typical Hitler fashion, the bulk of his own warmth appears to have been reserved, not for his comrades, but for his beloved dog. There was no doubt that Hitler absolutely doted upon Foxl (Foxy) a little white terrier who deserted from the British lines and attached himself to Hitler and whose devotion seems to have been totally reciprocated. Long after the Great War, on the night of 22nd-23rd January 1942, Hitler told the story of his favourite companion during one of his late night rambling monologues which was recorded by Bormann and later collected together and published as 'Hitler's Table Talk' by Sir Hugh Trevor Roper:

'It was in January 1915 that I got hold of Foxl. He was engaged in pursuing a rat that had jumped into our trench. He fought against me, and tried to bite me, but I didn't let go. I led him back with me to the rear. He constantly tried to escape. With exemplary patience (he didn't understand a word of German), I gradually got him used to me. At first I gave him only biscuits and chocolate (he'd acquired his habits with the English, who were better fed than we were). Then I began to train him. He never went an inch from my side. At that time, my comrades had no use at all for him. Not only was I fond of the beast, but it interested me to study his reactions. I finally taught him everything: how to jump over obstacles, how to climb up a ladder and down again. The essential thing is that a dog should always sleep beside its master. When I had to go up into the line, and there was a lot of shelling, I used to tie him up in the trench. My comrades told me that he took no interest in anyone during my absence. He would

recognise me even from a distance. What an outburst of enthusiasm he would let loose in my honour! We called him Foxl.'

Hitler clearly had a great attachment to his little companion and from his misty eyed recollection some 25 years later it seems to have been one of the most important and memorable relationships which he formed during the Great War.

Meanwhile the unremitting grind of trench warfare continued and a key witness to the next phase of the war was Private Westenkirchner who recalled the next episode in Hitler's war. The List Regiment, in the wake of the Battle of Neuve Chapelle, took up new positions in a fairly quiet sector of the Front which was to become a second home to Hitler and his comrades:

'After a time, the regiment found itself in Tourcoing, and then, in the spring, of 1915 when the British offensive hurled itself against Neuve Chapelle, we moved up in that direction, and occupied trenches in the neighbourhood of Fromelles. Here we remained, more or less, until the following autumn. As I said, Hitler and I were Meldegänger. For the sake of mobility we carried no arms except a small revolver. Our despatch wallets were attached to our belts. Generally two of us were sent out together, each bearing the same despatches, in case anything happened to the one or the other. The despatches were always sealed and marked with one, two or three crosses, according as they required time, haste, or express speed. It was no joke this despatch bearing, especially as Fromelles stood on a bit of a height, and to reach it from the troops in the plains and valleys below we had to toil up slopes raked by the enemy's machine-gun fire every inch of the way. I can see Hitler before my eyes now, as he used to tumble down back into the dug-out after just such a race with death. He'd squat down in a corner just as if nothing'd happened, but he looked a sketch - thin as a rake, hollow-eyed and waxy white.'

Somehow Hitler survived the gruelling ordeal described by Westenkirchner and the arrival of the fine summer weather at last provided some respite from the misery produced by the mud of winter and spring 1915, but the ever present danger from shelling meant that

Hitler and his colleagues had to spend a great deal of their time in one of the concrete bunkers which still dot the landscape around the small town of Fromelles. The fighting around Ypres was also characterised by mining and countermining which could result in a sudden and deadly explosion at any moment. Ignatz Westenkirchner again takes up the saga of the many forms of death which might await the participants in Hitler's war:

'It was pretty beastly in those dug-outs all that summer. I shall never forget it. Nothing got on a man's nerves more than to have the ground blow up right under his feet. You never knew whether or not you were sitting bang on top of a powder magazine. Suddenly there'd come the most sickening sensation as a mine was sprung, and the next thing you'd know was that ten or twenty of your pals and comrades, chaps who'd been at your elbow only a minute before, were flying around in ten thousand bloody bits. That wanted some sticking, I can tell you! By September the English were pressing the attack all along our Front harder and harder. On the night of the 25th September 1915 our position was pretty precarious; it seemed as if something decisive one way or the other must at last come off. The air was full of the screaming of shells and of the hideous hissing and crashing of the whizz-bangs. Suddenly our Company Officer discovered that telephonic communication with the next section had broken down, and Hitler and another man got the order to go and find out what was wrong. They made it somehow, but only got back by the skin of their teeth utterly done in. The wire had been cut: an attack in force was imminent. Warnings must be sent further afield. Hitler received the order a second time. It was nothing less than a miracle how he escaped with his life as he came out on the road between Fromelles and Aubers. It was literally raining shells. The attack, however, failed. How we withstood it I can't tell. I only thought to myself at the time how lucky our English and Indian prisoners ought to think themselves to be out of such a hell.'

The British attack which took place on 25th of September 1915 in the Fromelles sector burned itself into the memory of the men of the

List Regiment who were by now officially dubbed the 16th RIR. From their positions at Fromelles, Hitler and Schmidt, who were sent out to reconnoitre, brought back the disconcerting news that the British had secretly brought a number of large cylinders to the Front. With the wind blowing towards the 16th RIR positions, there was the imminent danger of a British gas-attack. At this difficult juncture Hitler was again sent out to reconnoitre, this time he took with him Balthasar Brandmayer. The two made their reconnaissance and were heading back to make their report at Regimental H.Q., when the messengers were caught in the middle of a heavy British barrage. The terrifying incident was later described in detail by Balthasar Brandmayer:

> 'Stones and iron fragments whizzed above our heads. We bent low, racing across open country. I could scarcely lift myself from the ground any more (and) still Hitler urged me onwards, onwards! I cannot understand how Hitler could look around, with no cover… while calling to me: "Brandmoari, get up!" He seemed without nerves…. Sweat dug deep rivulets into our faces. More falling than running, we reached the command dugout. Paralyzing tiredness weighed like lead on my burning limbs. I threw off my helmet and webbing and sank, dead-tired, into my bunk. I expected Adolf to do the same, but how wrong I was! As I turned around, I saw him sitting near the exit, helmet on head, buckled up, and waiting for the next order. "You're crazy!" I cried out angrily. "How would you know?" was his prompt reply. There was no man under his uniform, only a skeleton…. He had an iron nature.'

- CHAPTER 6 -

HITLER AT WAR

HITLER CERTAINLY COMMANDED THE admiration of many of those around him, but it was frequently a qualified admiration. Hitler it seemed was always too ready to launch into political tirades. He frowned on coarse soldiers talk concerning women, objected to smoking, cursing and was curiously reluctant to leave the front. Hitler gave ready voice to his strong support for the war and these opinions certainly did not endear him to those who hated the war and wanted it over, win or lose. Alexander Moritz Frey, then a young medical orderly in the German trenches during World War I, experienced one of Hitler's diatribes at first hand and, as he recorded the episode in his unpublished essay on Hitler, his first impressions of the man were very far from favourable:

'One evening a pale, tall man tumbled down into the cellar after the first shells of the daily evening attack had begun to fall. Fear and rage were glowing in his eyes. At that time he looked tall, because he was so thin. A full moustache... covered the ugly slit of his mouth. He sat there panting... His yellow face grew red... and he resembled a gobbling turkey as he began to rant about the English... I immediately had the same impression that many had of him later - that he responded to the military actions of the enemy at a personal level, as if they wanted to take his precious life in particular.'

From Frey's account it would appear that, even in the trenches, Hitler's fevered brain was in its usual torment. In the pages of *'Mein Kampf'* Hitler later recorded many of the issues which troubled him during his years of service at the Front and from the length of the diatribe our sympathies must go out to Frey and the others who had to endure these outpourings. Hitler later claimed that during the Great War he considered himself exclusively to be first and foremost a soldier who did not wish to meddle in politics on the grounds that he felt the time was simply inopportune. For that reason Hitler tells us he detested political agitators at the Front, whom he dubbed barrack room 'parliamentaries'. Hitler expressed his belief that the most modest 'stable-boy' served his country better than the 'parliametarians'. It is clear that Hitler strived to do his duty in an obsessive manner which was not at all characteristic of the average rank and file who inevitably gravitate towards performing on the bare minimum required. Hitler objected to barrack room lawyers and believed fervently that all decent men who had anything to say should say it in his words 'point-blank in the enemy's face'; or failing this, they should keep their mouths shut and do their duty. Hitler stated that, if he had his way, he would have all malcontents formed into a labour battalion which would have provided them with the opportunity of babbling amongst themselves to their hearts' content, without giving offence or doing harm to 'decent people'.

Despite the clear recollections of those serving alongside him that Hitler was inclined to launch into long meandering political monologues, by the time that he came to write 'Mein Kampf', Hitler appears to have developed selective amnesia. In his book he maintains the frankly untenable position that throughout the Great War he was solely concerned with soldiering:

> 'In those days I cared nothing for politics; but I could not help forming an opinion on certain manifestations which affected not only the whole nation but also us soldiers in particular. There were two things which caused me the greatest anxiety at that time and which I had come to regard as detrimental to our interests.'

We know enough of Hitler to be certain that he would have voiced this opinion loud and hard, not surprisingly there were those who gave him credit for his soldiering skills, but detested the political hectoring. Given all Hitler had to say about the long hours of political research which he claims to have undertaken in Vienna between 1908 and 1912 it is most unlikely that Hitler himself was not in fact one of the trench 'parliamentarians' whom he claimed to despise. Even

Ignatz Westenkirchner, who agrees with Hitler in almost every detail concerning his war service, could not provide any corroboration on this point, in fact his recollections as he recounted them to Heinz A. Heinz are the exact opposite of Hitler's stated case.

'For the most part he was always on about politics. Two things seemed to get his goat - what the papers were saying at home about the War and all, and the way the Government, and particularly the Kaiser, were hampered by the Marxists and the Jews. It was pretty plain, he said, what the working classes thought about "Socialism" when the War broke out. They just chucked it clean overboard, and joined up to a man. Then, again, it didn't need all that shouting in the papers whenever we gained a victory: it stood to reason that the German Army was equal to its job. Nor did the folk at home need to have their courage damped when things didn't look so well. Going on like that would sooner or later only lead to public indifference about the War altogether. As for the Kaiser encouraging the Marxists, they'd only take advantage of that, to stab the Army in the back.'

Even if we are to believe Hitler's debatable claim that he 'cared nothing for politics' there is no questioning the fact that his experiences in the Great War contributed strongly to Hitler's political awakening. It was in the trenches that he began to fully comprehend the power of the press to shape mass opinion. This development was noted and later communicated by Ignatz Westenkirchner to Heinz A Heinz:

'It was in the summer of 1915 that the enemy began to drop bundles of leaflets into our trenches and behind our lines. This was their idea of making propaganda, sowing seeds of discontent and doubt in our minds as to what the fighting was about and how the Kaiser and not the German people was responsible for the War. At first we didn't pay much attention to them, but as time went on we'd read them just for something to do. Mostly we chucked them away. They dropped leaflets against the Prussians on us Bavarian chaps.... Hitler knew what they meant by that. He read the things seriously and thought a lot about it all. He seemed to think the English understood propaganda better than we did, and this leaflet dropping certainly did have its effect.*

Arguments got up. Grousing increased all along the line. The wet and the mud and the weariness, the filth, and the wretched grub were all bad enough, without the men forever scrapping about what the enemy thought fit to tell them. Hitler seemed to expect H.Q. would contradict it. But H.Q. never did. Nothing was done to counteract the bad effect among us of those enemy leaflets.

Another thing where we found we'd gone wrong - the humorous papers had always given us to understand there wasn't such a dolt on God's earth as the French or British soldier. Now we had to meet them, face to face, we knew a jolly sight better. They were men, and tremendous fighters. We knew, too, how it was all the other way about in France and England. The War propaganda there, making out we Germans were 'Huns' and savages, capable of every sort of crime, just stiffened the people up to go on. Hitler was bitter over this. The enemy was much cleverer than we were about propaganda. He only wished he could have a say himself! But Hitler then was a nobody like the rest of us, nothing but a man in the trenches.'

Hitler was an astute reader of public opinion and according to *'Mein Kampf'* his main concern was based on his own conviction that once public enthusiasm for the war was damped down, nothing could enkindle the same intensity of enthusiasm again. Hitler felt that public enthusiasm was equivalent to an intoxication which had to be maintained and constantly topped up. Without the unyielding support of a press corps dedicated to building an enthusiastic public spirit he felt it would not be possible for Germany to endure a struggle which made immense demands on what he described as the 'spiritual stamina' of the nation. Hitler felt that he was too well acquainted with the psychology of the broad masses not to know that appeals for calm are irreconcilable with maintaining public fervour at boiling point. In his eyes it was a crime not to have tried to raise the pitch of public enthusiasm still higher and he could not understand why the policy of damping the public spirit was allowed to take root.

The short passage from *'Mein Kampf'* in which he rails against those calling for public restraint with regard to victory celebrations says more about Hitler than many of his rambling monologues. The doom for the freedom of the German press was clearly spelled out in 1924 when Hitler was writing *'Mein Kampf'*. These are plainly the words of a sociopath his response to the gentlemen of the press is typically disproportionate and full of murderous intent. It is astonishing that such callous and totally overt statements should have been overlooked by so many people who later cast their votes for a man who would deprive them of their rights just as quickly as he advocated dealing summary justice to journalists with whom he disagreed.

'Instead of catching these fellows by their long ears and dragging them to some ditch and looping a cord around their necks, so that the victorious enthusiasm of the nation should no longer offend the aesthetic sensibilities of these knights of the pen, a general Press campaign was now allowed to go on against what was called 'unbecoming' and 'undignified' forms of victorious celebration.'

It was not just the attitude of the press which irritated Hitler, he was also incensed by the manner in which Marxism was widely regarded and accepted. The abolition of party distinctions during the War had made Marxism appear almost mild and moderate. For Hitler however this was the Jewish doctrine which was being expounded for the express purpose of leading humanity to its destruction and he did not miss an opportunity to harangue his colleagues along those lines.

Hitler recorded that shortly after the first series of victories he soon detected how a certain section of the Press already begun to throw what he called 'cold water', on the enthusiasm of the public. It is typical of Hitler's paranoic tendencies that he should spot plots and conspiracies where none appeared to exist to the rest of the world. Hitler felt that in the beginning this particular campaign was waged so assiduously that it was invisible to most people and only those such as Hitler with his fully function conspiracy radar was able to detect the first signs of a plot to undermine the victories won by the German army. He maintained that this subtle press campaign had been orchestrated under the mask of good intentions and carefully disguised under a spirit of best intentions. What alarmed Hitler was the fact that the public was being told through the pages of the press that big public celebrations in honour of the victories which had been won at such great cost were now out of place and were somehow not worthy expressions of the spirit of a great nation like Germany. Hitler sensed that there was a move afoot to down play the successes in which he had played his part. The press, it seemed to him, were relaying a common message which took the fortitude and valour of German soldiers for granted and cautioned against national outbursts of celebration. On the part of the press it was understood the need to gain favourable foreign opinion was a factor which supported calls for a quiet and sober form of celebration rather than scenes of wild jubilation. Hitler totally dismissed these considerations and sensed that the press had an unspoken agreement to remind Germans that this war was not the fault of Germany and that hence there need be no feeling of shame in declaring Germany's willingness to do her share towards effecting a peaceful understanding among the nations.

For all of these reasons, Hitler decided that the press had chosen to wage a campaign to convince the German people that it would not be wise to sully the 'radiant deeds' of the German army with unbecoming jubilation which the rest of the world would never understand or forgive. Hitler it seemed could clearly detect in the attitude of the press the first signs of the defeatist attitude which would lead to the *Dolchstoss;* the 'stab in the back' of November 1918.

During 1915, Hitler and his unit remained in positon around Fromelles and the landscape became as familiar as his own homeland, but winter in Flanders was the real enemy. The water table is very close to the surface and constant shelling produced an ocean of mud which was the mutual enemy of both the British and the Germans. It left its literal and metaphorical mark on all combatants and its unpleasant presence was recalled by Ignatz Westenkirchner.

'The second winter came along, and whatever trouble the enemy gave us, the water and the mud gave us a rare sight more. It's a marvel we weren't all drowned. We lived waterlogged. Whole sections of the trenches had to be evacuated altogether. The pumps couldn't make any impression on the water. It just gained all the time. When we weren't

carrying messages, Hitler and the rest and I, we were slopping about on the duck-boards baling with buckets. He'd carry on with the job long after everyone else was fed up with it, and had given it up in despair. There was no snow, but ceaseless rain filled all the shell-holes around with water so that the whole expanse of No Man's Land was pitted with hideous lakes and looked like anything on earth rather than a battlefield. One of our fellows had been hoping against hope for a spell of leave. In December that year things were a bit quiet on our sector, so he put in for his pass. They said he could go on leave for a fortnight if he could get anyone to work double tides and take his place. He didn't need to think that over twice. He knew that Adolf Hitler would do it for him.'

As the war dragged on, the List Regiment became Hitler's surrogate family, here he seems to have discovered a sense of belonging. Within the highly structured context of a military regime, the position of runner gave Hitler a measure of freedom to live life by his own rules. It was up to the runner to find the best route to get the message through to its recipient and Hitler seems to have relished the semi-autonomous life. He is described as having an innate sense for choosing the safe route through even the heaviest shelling, he had a nose for danger and seemed to have a sixth sense which forewarned him where and when a shell was about to fall. His near miraculous powers of survival soon earned him the nickname 'Lucky Linzer'. Ignatz Westenkirchner also testified to the positive attitude which seems to have marked Hitler's entire service in the Great War. One curious observation is the fact that Hitler routinely attended the religious services held by Father Norbert which, given his subsequent attitude towards the Roman Catholic church, is something of a revalation.

'Hitler was always the one to buck us up when we got down-hearted: he kept us going when things were at their worst - but he couldn't cook! That was the one thing he couldn't do. One thing we couldn't understand - the rest of us - Hitler he'd always attend church parade, even towards the end, when most of us had given all that up.'

Hitler's success in delivering even the most difficult messages and conspicuous devotion to duty had already brought him his first medal, the Iron Cross Second Class, and with it came the recognition he craved. Hitler had saved the life of his commanding officer and in the act he had conspicuously risked his own life in the face of intense enemy fire. There is no doubt that the award of the Iron Cross Second Class was well deserved, the attainment of which he described in a letter to Herr Popp as 'the happiest day of my life'. This small metal cross was a talisman, it provided overt recognition of everything Hitler believed in and encapsulated the values which he admired most; sacrifice, obedience, duty, discipline and loyalty to the Fatherland.

As autumn gave way to winter the List Regiment remained stuck in it's position around Fromelles. Ignatz Westenkirchner again takes up the narrative:

'Christmas came round again without any of us yet knowing how soon the war would be over, or how much more of it we'd got to face. It was pretty miserable, but they'd concocted some punch in the canteen, and at least every man had got letters or parcels from home. Everyone, that is, except Hitler. Somehow Hitler never got a letter even! It wasn't a thing that called for remark exactly. But we all felt sorry, inside, and wanted him to share and share alike with us. But he never would! Never accepted so much as a Kuchen! (cake). It was no use to keep all on at him. Not that he wasn't free-handed enough when he had anything of his own to share, a cigarette or bit of sausage. The measly pay we got he'd spend on jam. It was jam first and butter afterwards, that is whenever the two things did happen both to be within reach at the same time. It was bread and scrape anyhow, but Hitler, he was a rare one for jam!'

It was in the trenches and the ranks of the List Regiment in particular that Hitler was destined to meet many of the colleagues who would form the clique at the heart of the National Socialist movement. Fritz Wiedemann was one example and, although they did not fight together, Rudolf Hess, Hitler's future deputy, gained instant credit in Hitler's eyes on the grounds that Hess was a former soldier from the trenches. Max Amann was another future Nazi luminary who actually did come to know Hitler as a result of shared experiences during the Great War, although according to Moritz Frey their early relationship was less than cordial. One relationship which did endure was Hitler's friendship with Ignatz Wetenkircher and we are fortunate to have such a detailed and lengthy record of Hitler's service in the Great War.

'*The year wore on towards spring. The poor bits and stumps of trees left sticking up here and there like splintered posts in the mud actually began to put out leaves: sometimes a gleam of sun dried the morass a bit. Then the fighting renewed itself: new and terrific offensives developed all along the line. This was when the gas attacks began. The Battle of the Somme went on right through July without the enemy breaking our line anywhere. I shall never forget the night of the 15th or the 16th as long as I live. It was an inferno of fire. All our field telephones were out of action and we 'Meldegänger' were on the go incessantly, our lives at stake every moment. At one time we were opposed to Australians. They came on over and over again only to be mowed down by our machine-gun fire. News came that the enemy were breaking through the line held by the 21st Infantry Regiment: word had to be sent along to the 17th and then on to the threatened sector. Hitler and another trench runner got the order. They set off in the face of almost certain death, peppered with shot and shell every yard of the way. Half the time they were cowering for shelter in shell-holes and ditches. They were wet through and half-frozen. Hitler's companion gave out. Buckled right up, unable to stick it another step! Hitler hoisted him along somehow, rather than leave him to his fate, and the two of them came at last, God only knows how, back to the dug-out. On the 20th we delivered a counter-attack and wrested back again the few yards of trenches gained previously by the enemy. There came a bit of a lull after that and we runners did what we could to repair damage to our dug-out. Presently with over one hundred dead we marched into rest billets at Fournes.*'

Hitler had no way of knowing at the time, but the German army of the Great War was outmatched and outnumbered. With the notable exception of Verdun in 1916 and the *Kaiserschlacht* in 1918, there were no great German offensives in the west after 1914. The German army was able to survive by sitting on the defensive and attempting to grind down the allied will to fight on. Military technology had advanced sufficiently that the attacking force was placed at a complete disadvantage. Well planned and constructed defences, albeit at great cost, could generally thwart even the most dedicated attacker. It is important to note that Hitler's experiences in the trenches were therefore shaped almost completely by a long series of defensive actions from Aubers Ridge in 1915 through the great Somme Battles and the fighting around Arras. It was only in the spring of 1918 that Hitler was to experience again the brief exhilaration of a major German advance. The fact that Hitler had experienced so many defensive actions would have grave consequences for the German armies which he commanded in World War II. Based on his personal experiences in the trenches he formed the opinion that dogged determination to hold on at all costs could be a war winning strategy. It was to have grave consequences for the men of the Sixth Army at Stalingrad.

A noteable example of the dogged defence which the German army was called upon to provide, took place on 19th-20th July 1916 when the 16th RIR occupied the fortified position known as 'the sugarloaf'. They were subjected to a violent offensive by Australian troops who suffered catastrophic casualties in the attack. Hitler's fellow despatch runner, Balthasar Brandmayer, later described the course of yet another defensive battle:

'We carried message after message from and to the trenches. Glaring flares lit our way. The Australians stormed for the fifth time vainly across the battlefield. Those who escaped the rain of bullets from our machine-guns, found certain death in the hurricane of the German artillery fire.... I dashed with Hitler to the battle H.Q. of the 17th Regiment. He scarcely gave me time to get my breath back and we ran on to 21st Regiment. Grenades chased us through the darkness of the night; we rolled in time with them into a water-filled mine crater. The light of a high-flying flare first gave us an instance of orientation again. "Now push on!" said Hitler, and we scrambled up the crater *wall. Wet through to above the chest, our trousers and shirts stuck to our bodies. And how we froze! The envelope and paper we handed the regimental commander were soggy. He was scarcely able to decipher the report.'*

Despite the harrowing nature of the battle for the 'sugar loaf', Hitler was more content than at any time in his life. The small and close knit group of the List Regiment H.Q. provided a surrogate home and family, above all, he had a cause to which he could relate and a clear understanding that his service was a part of his duty to contribute to the success of the pan-German nationalist movement:

'I was now habitually calm and resolute. And that frame of mind endured. Fate might now put me through the final test without my nerves or reason giving way. The young volunteer had become an old soldier. This same transformation took place throughout the whole army. Constant fighting had aged and toughened it and hardened it, so that it stood firm and dauntless against every assault.'

The Australian-led attack of 19th and 20th July 1916 was an unusual event in the normally quiet Fromelles sector. The real nightmare for the German High Command and rank and file alike was the developing battle in Picardy which was to become known as the infamous Battle of the Somme. From the relative tranquility of Fournes, Hitler and the 16th RIR regiment were ordered in September 1916 to transfer to the Somme sector where the horrendous ordeal for the German army which had begun on 1st July 1916 was still continuing.

Hitler was certainly not destined to be promoted to the highly conservative and inward looking officer corps. He lacked the background, breeding and education for that, but the reason why a conspicuously brave soldier like Hitler failed to rise above the rank of Gefreiter is a question which has vexed historians for many years. Writing in the pages of *'Mein Kampf'* Hitler himself casts no light on the reason for his failure to progress through the ranks. One obvious reason might lie in the fact that he was not a German citizen and therefore not considered worthy of acceptance, but Sargeant Max Amann was interrogated on the subject after the war and he made it clear that although Hitler had been selected for promotion he had begged to be allowed to remain in his position as a Gefreiter. Interestingly, Heinz A. Heinz conducted a brief interview with Sargeant Max Amann on the same subject in 1934 and Amann's answer coincided with the answers Amann later gave to his US interrogators. It seemed that Hitler wished to remain in his relatively safe position as a regimental runner. This was certainly how Amann explained the situation to Heinz in 1934:

> 'Another comrade, Herr Max Amann, formerly regimental clerk, adds that Hitler never wanted a commission. He'd joined up in the ranks, and in the ranks he wanted to remain. "Often," he says, "Hitler would take another man's place, if he could - preferably a family man's - and volunteer for the extra dangerous job in his stead."'

There is no reason to doubt the fact that Hitler was the model of the courageous and dutiful soldier. As we have seen he had already won the Iron Cross Second Class by December 1914 and this was the beginning of an impressive list of awards and commendations. On 17th September 1917, he was awarded the Military Service Cross with swords; on May 9th 1918, he was awarded the regimental diploma 'for signal bravery in attack'; and on August 4th 1918, he received the Iron Cross, First Class. However, based on his own personal experience in the Great War, Moritz Frey came to the conclusion that, despite his obvious devotion to duty, Hitler was content to remain a corporal for the self same reason that Frey himself was happy to remain a medical assistant. The regimental runners were mainly engaged in running messages from Regimental H.Q., which could be five kilometers behind the lines, to the Battalion H.Q.s which might be two kilometres behind the lines. Unlike the company runners who served in the front line trenches, the regimental messengers were not routinely exposed to the dangers of life in the front line. It is ironic that those serving in the rear areas under the eye of the regimental staff were also more likely to obtain promotion, there were certainly fewer privations behind the lines and a far higher prospect of survival. In his unpublished essay, Moritz Frey was able to sum up the lot of the regimental courier from first hand experience:

'Compared to the terrible hardship of serving in the trenches and the correspondingly high mortality, a posting to a position behind the lines was a small improvement which came complete with small comfort.'

- CHAPTER 7 -

HITLER RUNS OUT OF LUCK

O N 4TH AUGUST 1942, AROUND MIDDAY, Hitler was holding forth in one of his rambling monologues known to posterity as Hitler's tabletalk and he recalled the scene as the 16th RIR arrived for the first time on the battlefields of the Somme. The regiment was to go into action near the town of Bapaume which was a hotspot in this most ferocious of battles:

'When we went into the line in 1916, to the south of Bapaume, the heat was intolerable. As we marched through the streets, there was not a house, not a tree to be seen; everything had been destroyed, and even the grass had been burnt. It was a veritable wilderness. Marching along the roads was a misery for us poor old infantrymen; again and again we were driven off the road by the bloody gunners, and again and again we had to dive into the swamps to save our skins! All the thanks we got was a torrent of curses "Bloody So-and-Sos" was the mildest expression hurled at us.'

At the time when Hitler and the 16th RIR were transferring to the Somme, Alexander Moritz Frey undertook the rail journey in the company of Private Hitler and the man who was then known as Sergeant Amann:

'I sat together with Max Amann and Hitler in the same train compartment… Hitler sat opposite us, sleeping with his mouth open. He slept with his chin hanging down and had stretched out his feet in such a way that Amann, with his short fat legs (he always had plenty to eat due to his connections) was wedged in. Amann gave the sleeping man a kick against the shinbone. Hitler gave a start. "Kindly keep your joints to yourself!" said the sergeant in a commanding tone.

Hitler understood, then he went red. For a moment he looked liked
he wanted to lunge at the other man, but immediately managed to
keep his temper under control and he said nothing. Amann said, in a
sarcastically pacifying tone, "Yes, I mean you, Private Hitler."'

They could not have known it at the time but Hitler and the men of the 16th RIR were marching into the gates of Hell. They were about to face an ordeal which made all of their previous trials seem mild by comparison. The Battle of the Somme, was a long-drawn-out affair. It lasted, in fact, some three and a half months, from 1st July 1916 well on into the autumn. The battle is often considered solely from the Britsh perspective but it was in fact an allied offensive and was planned on a single front of about twenty-five miles and was preceded by immense preparations and reinforcements in men and material. The French were initially successful but despite some small gains amounting to around eight miles the British failed to break the German line. The reason was, of course, that the German lines consisted of an entire belt of territory scored with lines behind lines, every one of which had to be taken and cleared and held before the British could be said to have broken through.

The British failed to do so and at frightful cost and over two months were spent in trying to secure objectives marked down for the first day or two of the battle: it took weeks upon weeks to decide the possession of a single patch of woodland; prolonged struggles waged backwards and forwards over a few metres of contested ground. The futility of the German attack on Verdun was balanced by the desperate defence of Bapaume. The Somme, even more than Verdun, was to prove the crucible which ultimately ground down the German army. The flow of losses which began on 1st July 1916 were irreplaceable. During their short ten day spell in the lines near Bapaume, the 16th RIR suffered 120 casualties for every day. Ignatz Westenkirchner naturally recalled the awful reality of the fighting as experienced by both he and Adolf Hitler:

'That Somme Battle, a witches' cauldron of horror and fire and
death, went on for weeks. Some time before we'd all been issued with
fresh equipment. Now, on the 25th of September, we were marched off
to Haubourdin, there to entrain next day for Longwy. From there we

*marched endlessly it seemed to us through Cambrai to Fremicourt,
where we set to work at top speed to dig ourselves in, constructing
trenches, traverses and dug-outs day and night. We took part in the
battle on the 2nd of October and found ourselves in the sector between
Bapaume and La Barque. It was all new ground to us, and we
messengers were lost half the time. We relieved the 21st Regiment. The
men came straggling back scarcely recognisable in their mud, blood
and rags. Once a shell dropped plump into the middle of our dug-
out. For the moment the lot of us were too stunned to know what
had happened. Then we saw four of us lay dead, and seven others lay
hideously wounded spouting blood on the ground. That was the first
time Hitler caught one. A splinter had gashed him in the face.'*

Balthasar Brandmayer was another of Hitler's colleagues who
recorded his impressions of the horrendous ordeal which the Imperial
German Army was forced to endure on the Somme battlefield:

*'There were dead and buried everywhere. We fell from shell hole
to shell hole. Multicolored flares arched heavenwards, and burst into
countless streams. This was always the moment after which we leapt for
another freshly turned-up crater in which to disappear. Shrapnel, filth
and iron rained mercilessly down on us. The blood almost stagnated
in my arteries, it could only be a few seconds longer - then, yes - then
an armored-steel force ripped at bodies already scratched and torn.
My nerve failed. I just wanted to lie where I was, I sank hopelessly
into insupportable apathy…. Then Hitler spoke kindly to me, gave
me words of encouragement, said that someday all our heroism would
be rewarded a thousand fold in the Fatherland…. We returned…
uninjured. Our faces were no longer recognizable.'*

Not surprisingly with the constant presence of death just around the
corner, even Hitler would eventually use up his store of good fortune.
However even in the face of such overpowering danger Hitler continued
to do his duty. Ignatz Westenkirchner was another Lister who vividly
recalled the terrible events which were played out on the battlefield of
the Somme:

'On the night of the 5th and 6th of October 1916 Hitler was on

the go with messages between our lot and the 17th the whole time. For the most part he and his comrade were dodging high explosive in the open, just waiting between earthquakes and volcanoes to make the next bit there and back. The enemy was doing his utmost to smash the German line, but in spite of unprecedented ferocity, the attack was completely foiled. We didn't give way an inch. By day we lay as close underground as we could. Otherwise, the slightest sign of life on our part brought the enemy aeroplanes into play and bombs were dropped right from overhead. Of an evening, as a rule, Hitler was despatched to Brigade Headquarters at Bapaume. To get there he ran such a gauntlet between exploding mines and burning houses, that for the most part his own clothes singed on his back. Over and over again the company was only saved by our artillery from the English onslaughts.'

On 12th October 1916, Lucky Linzer finally ran out of the commodity that had sustained him for over two years of war. While on duty near the town of Bapaume during the Battle of the Somme he was wounded in either the groin area or the left thigh. The aftermath of the incident was witnessed by Ignaz Westenkirchner:

'From the 7th of October for five days and nights it isn't too much to say that we trench runners got no sleep and nothing but snatch grub to eat. Our numbers grew ever fewer and fewer. The stunning din in the air never let up for one moment. All was the wildest uproar of death by shot and shell and cannonade. The thing grew unendurable, not to be believed. It took six runners now to get a message through, three pairs of them set out on the off chance that one man, perhaps, might succeed. Our Lieutenant called for volunteers - only Hitler responded, and a chap named Ernst Schmidt. The thing was rank suicide. This time only Schmidt got back. Hitler had been hit in the left leg. Later on the regimental stretcher-bears brought him in. They took us out of the line on the 13th of October. Only a handful of us, apathetic with shock and exhaustion, stumbled off, making our way as best we could over the corpses of our comrades.'

According to Private Westenkirchner, the battle of attrition which the British generals had planned for was beginning to take it's toll:

'The companies got smaller and smaller; hardly thirty men went to a company now. And in this shape we awaited new onslaughts. The bombardment was incessant. At length, however, we went into rest billets at Sancourt.'

As the days passed it became evident that although Hitler's wound was serious enough to merit a spell in hospital, it was not so severe as to incapacitate him permanently, but it was certainly enough to disable him for some months and would require a period of convalescence. Accordingly he was sent to the rear to the *'Sammellazarett'* Hermies where he appears to have undergone some dental work probably as result of the facial wound he had received. Writing in 'Germany's Hitler' Heinz A. Heinz affords us a fairly accurate account of the next chapter of the war as provided by Ignatz Westenkirchner which veers suspiciously close to the version of events described in *'Mein Kampf'*.

'For two long years he had been at the Front: here, for the first time in all that while, he heard a German woman's voice again. It was that of the Sister at the Base Hospital. It gave him quite a shock. But he went on in the Ambulance Train, through Belgium, back home to Germany - after two years! It was amazing at last to find himself, clean, and lying in a soft white bed in hospital at Beelitz near Berlin. He had become so unused to all this refinement! It took him quite a while to get accustomed to these new surroundings. The thing, though, that struck him most, back there at home in hospital, was the demoralisation that seemed to have got hold of the men. There were chaps there making a boast of how they'd purposely maimed themselves to get out of the fighting line, and, what was a jolly sight worse, no one in authority took notice of it, no one seemed to think the less of them for it. What they said was 'Better to play the coward for a minute than to be dead for eternity.' Everybody was grousing over the beastliness of the Front, and the uselessness of the war in general. Hitler could hardly believe his ears. It might have been true, but it was unworthy and unsoldierly.'

Hitler was ill at ease in hospital and he sent a number of postcards to his colleagues at the front complaining of the tribulations caused by his dental treatment. We are fortunate to have a glimpse of his sense of humour in the post card which he sent to Balthasar Brandmeyer.

'Am suffering from hunger-induced typhus, because I cannot eat bread; additionally, I am adamantly denied any sort of jam.'

Ignatz Westenkirchner followed Hitler's progress and was later able to recall the events for Heinz A. Heinz. He picks up the narrative as Hitler is once again becoming mobile:

'Then one day, when he was fairly convalescent, he got leave to go to Berlin. Everything there looked baddish, he thought; poverty and hunger and anxiety were stamped on every face. He went into one or two of the Soldiers' Homes, but found the chaps there much in the same frame of mind as in the hospital, only worse. The grousers seemed to have it all their own way. Hitler felt pretty sick I can tell you....'

Once he had recovered from his wound, Hitler was posted to a replacement battalion away from the trenches. He hated the time spent in Munich which was the city which Hitler now called home. His period of rest was a shock and he was dismayed by the lack of popular support for the war. Hitler's wound may well have saved his life. He spent one of the most difficult and testing times in the entire history of the regiment in a rear area hospital. The Battle of the Somme was to prove one of the most difficult ordeals in the long litany of misery for the List Regiment. By 1917 when Hitler had fully recovered, the List Regiment had served its time on the Somme and Heinz A. Heinz recorded the undimmed enthusiasm of Adolf Hitler as he returned to duty in the months which would see the build up to the Battle of Arras. It is interesting to note that the 1937 English translation of 'Germany's Hitler' correctly avoids describing Hitler as a corporal and translates Gefreiter as Lance-Corporal.

'Lance-Corporal Adolf Hitler (as he was now) had, indeed, come back from the Front (as he was to emerge from the War at the end), with all his ideals and loyalties intact. He had gone from the high untried courage of the beginning through shock and horror and exhaustion to admitted cowardice and fear, but this in turn he had *conquered and steeled to dogged endurance. It had never yet entered his head to start malingering; or to question the obvious tightness of the War. He was utterly disgusted by all this, back in Berlin.*

When he was fit for discharge, the "iron train", which carried men on leave, took him to his Reserve Battalion in Munich. Here things were no better than in Berlin. Glowering faces, grumbling speech, and incessant invective against Prussians and militarism were to be noted on every hand. Hitler couldn't make it out how all this seemed to have got up, and got up so suddenly. He found out, however, that a lot of newspaper men having gone to the Front, their places had been taken by Jews, and that these men were using their opportunity to foment discouragement and disunion. Everything tracked to a nicety with the enemy propaganda in the trenches. If the Bavarians and the Prussians could be brought to loggerheads, so much the better for those who would like to see both go under.'

It is apparent that by 1917 the home situation was so desperate and gloomy that Hitler would do anything to escape that dismal state of affairs and return to the front where he would still at least be fighting for Germany. Hitler was clearly very unhappy to be away from the Front, he had made a place for himself in that world. He was valued and respected and he had no other desire in life than to return to his comrades. In a badly spelt postcard dated 19th December 1916 from Hitler to his regimental comrade Karl Lanzhammer, who at this time was a bicycle courier at regimental headquarters of the 16th Bavarian Reserve Infantry Regiment, he informed Lanzhammer that he was now with the Reserve Battalion, and was still undergoing dental treatment and would as soon as possible voluntarily report back to the field. In the brief text, Hitler reveals some of his characteristic spelling difficulties by rendering the German word for immediately, *(sofort)* with double f – 'soffort':

'Dear Lanzhammer, I am now in Munich at the Reserve Battalion. Currently I am under dental treatment. By the way I will report voluntarily for the field immediately.

Kind regards A. Hitler'

- CHAPTER 8 -

1917 - THE RETURN TO THE FRONT

HITLER INTENDED TO RETURN TO HIS familiar role in the ranks of the 16th RIR, however there was a shock in store for him when he discovered that he was due to be posted to the ranks of the 2nd Infantry Regiment, which was a regular formation. The upshot of it all was that Hitler himself lobbied hard to return to the Front and to the welcoming embrace of his old regiment. He knew he had to act fast if he was ever to be re-united with his colleagues and his faithful Foxl. He petitioned by letter to be allowed to return to the ranks of the List Regiment and finally got his wish by being granted permission to return to his old position and re-joining the 16th RIR at the front in March 1917.

Ignatz Westenkirchner was one of those who was pleased to see the return of a valued and esteemed comrade:

'We chaps in the line were glad to have him back, I can tell you. He was one of the best comrades we ever had. The company cook excelled himself that night and turned out an extra special mess in his honour, Kartoffelpuffer, bread and jam and tea. Hitler was cheery, too. Long after the rest of us had turned in, he was still fooling about with a flashlight in the dark spitting the rats on his bayonet. Then somebody chucked a boot at his head, and we got a little peace.'

Also waiting for Hitler was his faithful little terrier Foxl. The small white dog is pictured in many of the snaps for which Hitler and his colleagues posed in the garden of their comfortable billet in Fournes during 1916. Karl Lanzhammer, another of Hitler's long term comrades, had looked after the dog while his owner was away in hospital. The long overdue meeting which took place between Hitler and Foxl in March 1917 was a moment of great importance for him and the warm memory of that special occasion remained with him even after he had become the *Fürher*. Over twenty years later in his table talk monologue which was recorded by Martin Bormann at mid-day on 23rd January 1942, Hitler fondly recalled their happy reunion:

'He went through all the Somme, the Battle of Arras. He was not at all impressionable. When I was wounded, it was Karl Lanzhammer who took care of him. On my return, he hurled himself on me in frenzy. When a dog looks in front of him in a vague fashion and with clouded eyes, one knows that images of the past are chasing each other through his memory. How many times, at Fromelles, during the first World War, I've studied my dog Foxl. When he came back from a walk with the huge bitch who was his companion, we found him covered with bites. We'd no sooner bandaged him, and had ceased to bother about him, than he would shake off this unwanted load. A fly began buzzing. Foxl was stretched out at my side, with his muzzle between his paws. The fly came close to him. He quivered, with his eyes as if hypnotised. His face wrinkled up and acquired an old man's expression. Suddenly he leapt forward, barked and became agitated. I used to watch him as if he'd been a man - the progressive stages of his anger, of the bile that took possession of him. He was a fine creature. When I ate, he used to sit beside me and follow my gestures with his gaze. If by the fifth or sixth mouthful I hadn't given him anything, he used to sit up on his rump and look at me with an air of saying: "And what about me, am I not here at all?" It was crazy how fond I was of the beast. Nobody could touch me without Foxl's instantly becoming furious. He would follow nobody but me. When gas-warfare started, I couldn't go on taking him into the front line. It was my comrades who fed him. When I returned after two days' absence, he would refuse to leave me again. Everybody in the trenches loved him. During marches he would run all round us, observing everything, not missing a detail. I used to share everything with him. In the evening he used to lie beside me.'

Besides re-familiarising himself with his faithful terrier, Hitler in early 1917 also had to quickly get back into the routine of soldiering. From the German perspective, this once more involved fighting doggedly on the defensive against a well supplied and well fed allied force which was growing stronger and bolder with every month which passed. The terrible effects of the blockade were slowly strangling Germany into submission and the Imperial German Army was beginning to show the strain of a war which could never be won. The next allied blow was about to fall at Arras and Ignatz Westenkirchner supplied the detail of the course of battle over the next few months in his 1934 interview with Heinz A. Heinz.

'On March 4th 1917 we left and entrained, via Douai, for Hantay on the La Bassée Canal. Things were gingering up and we were preparing for the big spring offensive at Arras. By 28th April 1917 we were in position at Biache. There was nothing to see but a waste of water-logged shell-holes. On 3rd May we were in action at Roeux; and five days later we relieved the 20th, in the middle of a gas attack from the English. The effect of it was appalling. We messengers had a severe time of it, continually under fire, rain in our faces cutting like knives, mud up to our knees. The earth was going up in cascades all about us; we continually fell headlong into shell-holes old and new. The company got scattered anyhow; many of them never turned up again. Hitler and the rest were kept hard at it all night. At one time they were within an inch of capture by the English.'

By July 1917 the ordeal of the Battle of Arras was over for the List Regiment, which was once more transferred to the familiar world of the Ypres salient. By now the little town and the surrounding villages had witnessed almost three years of constant warfare and as a result the landscape had changed beyond all recognition. Despite all that they had endured to date, Ignatz Westenkirchner hailed the return to Ypres as an even worse chapter than either the Somme or Arras. This gives us an idea of just how difficult the fighting was in the Ypres salient.

'But Ypres was the worst experience of all. Fifteen hundred strong the List Regiment was moved up into the salient on 13th July 1917.

We had come by night from Roulers to Ledeghem; from there we marched via Terhand to Gheluveld. All this was covering old ground for us, but it was no longer recognisable. We saw nothing but ruined villages, whole towns lying in masses of rubble, the very configuration of the streets all gone, here and there a gaunt and jagged gable still gaped to the sky.

Then for ten days and nights on end we were bombarded without pause or slackening. There was the sound underground of mining and boring, and fleets of war planes rained bombs from overhead. For twenty-four hours at a stretch we suffocated in our gas masks. Then three days of rest billets in Dadizeele. Then in the line again between Gheluveld and Becelaire.

On 31ˢᵗ July 1917 the English brought their monsters of tanks into action over a frontage miles long. They were accompanied overhead by planes, and heralded by intense machine-gun fire. Our artillery checked their advance. The rain foiled them still worse. It came down the whole time as if the heavens had opened. The field of battle was turned into one vast flooded area in which the enemy tanks were useless, and men and horses on either side were in as much danger of being drowned as shot. It went on, like a second deluge, for four days and nights, and was succeeded by weather black as winter.'

This appalling experience in the Ypres salient was almost beyond endurance but every nightmare has to end sometime. Eventually the 16th RIR was withdrawn from the hot-spot around Ypres and allocated to a quiet sector of the line in Alsace which was the only part of the line where the lines of the trenches actually encroached into Germany itself. For Adolf Hitler and the worn out men of the 16th RIR this was to prove a novelty from both the geographical location, and also the relative peace and calm of the battlefield. For both reasons the posting was warmly recalled by Ignatz Westenkirchner:

'Anyhow, Regiment List was sent southward for a spell, to Hochstadt, near Muhlhausen in Alsace. After Flanders this was a foretaste of paradise!'

While Westenkirhner was in raptures over the List Regiment's new posting to a quiet sector of the front, it was to prove an absolute disaster for Hitler. During the train journey Foxl, his faithful little companion, was stolen by a railway official. Hitler seems to have been unmoved by the terrible human pain and suffering which was all around him, but the theft of his dog was a catastrophe. The loss was to trouble Hitler for the next twenty odd years and he bitterly recalled the whole incident to his audience in January 1942:

> 'To think that they stole him from me! I'd made a plan, if I got out of the war alive, to procure a female companion for him. I couldn't have parted from him. I've never in my life sold a dog. Foxl was a real circus dog. He knew all the tricks. I remember, it was before we arrived at Colmar. The railway employee who coveted Foxl came again to our carriage and offered me two hundred marks. "You could give me two hundred thousand, and you wouldn't get him!" When I left the train at Harpsheim, I suddenly noticed that the dog had disappeared. The column marched off, and it was impossible for me to stay behind! I was desperate. The swine who stole my dog doesn't realise what he did to me.'

- CHAPTER 9 -

THE KAISERSCHLACHT

THE SPELL IN THE TRENCHES AROUND Hochstadt, near Muhlhausen was a blessing for the men of the 16th RIR, they could take the opportunity to rest, build up their strength and gather their energies for the renewed challenges ahead. This much needed period of respite in a quiet sector was to prove disappointly short. The List Regiment had only a couple of month's rest before they went into the line again near Lizy on the Aisne.

The fighting here was dogged and obstinate and lasted practically all that winter as the months dragged round from 1917 into 1918. At the end of January 1918 however, there was at last some good news, and the 16th RIR was withdrawn to Gommines for another spell of rest. Balthasar Brandmayer joyfully recalled the much needed period of rest which was relished by the exhausted men:

'What a wonderful time! Misery and need are quickly forgotten. Anxiety and fear, through the long war years, have become unknown conceptions. So the visits, each day, of aviators dropping bombs does not disrupt in the least our royal Bavarian rest. Hitler saw a letter from my girlfiend and asked in a good-humored tone: "Brandmoari, has Trutschnelda written again?" "Good guess", I retorted. "Have you never wanted a girl?" I asked. "Look Brandmoari, I've never found time for such a thing," Hitler replied. "And I don't want to," he continued. "You're a strange one, Adi! I'll never understand you," I replied. "There's no hope for you." "How would it be if I found a mam'selle for us?" someone asked... "I'd kill myself from shame rather than make love to a French woman", Hitler leapt excitedly into the discussion. The effect of the moment was raucous laughter. "Listen to

the monk!" cried one. Hitler's face became serious. "Don't any of you feel your honour as a German any more?"'

Despite the odd moment of tension among the runners, for once there was good news on the military front too. There were stunning German successes to report from the Italian front and there was even better news as Tsarist Russia collapsed and descended into revolution. On 3rd March 1918 the Treaty of Brest-Litovsk marked the exit of Russia from the Great War. These strategic developments would allow the German High Command enough resources to make one last throw of the dice on the Western Front and it would involve the List regiment in some of the hardest fighting of the whole war. Ignatz Westenkirchner recalled how Adolf Hitler remained in tune with the bigger strategic picture:

'Hitler's interest in things in general never dwindled away to just concern for nothing more than what the day brought forth. That winter of 1917 the Russian Front buckled up, which was an immense thing for us, and so did the Italian; but then came the munitions strike at home. For three long years we'd held the Russian hordes at bay on the east. Endless columns of Russian prisoners swarmed over the high roads in Germany and yet there seemed to be illimitable numbers yet to come. It seemed almost laughable to us that the German Army, strung out on half a dozen fronts, should hope to resist this perennial flood. It held out successfully until the events of this winter allowed us to concentrate on the west. For the first time it almost looked as though we could change over from a war of defence to one of attack. The spirits of the men went up, and one even heard snatches of song again in the trenches. We got the idea that the enemy was losing heart: it could only now be a matter of one last terrific effort, before they, too, collapsed like Russia. As the spring advanced it was pretty plain they were jumpy and uneasy in those opposite trenches.

Then came the munitions strike at home, the most incredible bit of treachery and knavery the world has ever seen. The German Army was knifed in the back. The lives of hundreds and thousands of our men yet to be slaughtered were to lie at the doors of those who fomented and engineered this monstrous treason. Although the strike was called off too soon for the effects of it, as far as armaments were concerned, to be much felt at the Front, the consequences on our morale were deadly. Everyone began to ask what was the good of our carrying on out here if the people at home had thrown up the sponge? The Army began to be divided against itself. The enemy wasn't slow to take advantage of all this. They peppered our lines again with propaganda leaflets: 'Germany in the throes of a general strike,' 'Give it up: we've won.' Nevertheless, somehow, we fought on.'

The Imperial German Army did indeed fight on, and reinforced by the influx of men from the Russian front there was just about enough man-power for a last desperate lunge at her enemies. This was the *Kaiserschlacht*, the great spring offensive of March 1918 and initially, at least, the German Armies advanced with their morale raised at the prospect of a war-winning attack. Balthasar Brandmayer recalled the new found mood of optimism.

'We all felt within us the approach of the long-desired peace. Peace - the tug of the homeland - already these thoughts in themselves gave us courage and the confidence to endure patiently the few months that the war on the battlefields of France would perhaps still last. With songs of home on their lips again, for the first time in years, the fighting battalions of the glorious List Regiment pushed on.'

This last desperate effort began when the German armies once more gathered their strength to take the offensive. Ignatz Westenkirchner served alongside Hitler during those tumultuous months of the *Kaiserschlacht* which saw the Germans seize the initiative and break the Britsh and French lines. By 1918 the armies on both sides were unaccustomed to having to advance over long distances and although Hitler was noted for his physical endurance anyone would be taxed to the limit by the demanding marches described by Westenkirchner:

'On the 15th March 1918 our big offensive opened in Champagne and we succeeded in retaking a good slice of the country from the enemy. The battle was waged without cessation day or night; from a huge defensive action between Soissons and Reims it gradually

involved the whole Front from the Marne to the Aisne. The barrage was unintermittent. For fourteen days shot and shell rained on the trenches. We crouched in a veritable hell of fire and flying iron. We List fellows evacuated our old position on the Oise-Aisne sector, and pushed forward on a four-day long march which I shall never forget. Forty miles covered, every day of it, and this over roads you couldn't call roads any longer, they were so ploughed and shot to pieces. We had to make way all along the march for endless trains of munition waggons, and the incessant struggling forward of heavy artillery. Every now and again the whole advance would be held up by some heavy trench mortar having got stuck in a shell-hole. Horses had to be taken from the limbers of the other guns to try and haul it out, and masses of men turned to lend a hand. A dozen or so gunners hauling on long ropes, a grey coil of exhausted men, would bow forward at the word of command, 'Heave,' and strain till the sweat poured down their powder-blackened faces, while the horses floundered up to their bellies in the mud. If at last the monster at which they pulled reared itself by degrees out of the hole, there might be some chance of getting forward again. In silence and haste we struggled forward, our wide coats flapping and waving, with the belts unfastened, the covers of our helmets all in rags. By evening, one day, we reached Fourdrain. We camped three nights in the open air and did fifty miles at a stretch. The horses of the batteries ahead went down literally in dozens, and had to be summarily put out of their misery. We marched on through heaps of unrecognizable ruins, once villages, past La Fere, Vouel and Noyen, themselves nothing but burnt and shattered shells. On the third day we came to Lassigny and Amy. The farther ahead we pushed the more cumbered grew the way with the corpses of shot horses and the wreckage of heavy ordinance.

The French made terrific efforts to hold Montdidier; they hurled their coloured troops into the battle here. After indescribable struggles on 28th March 1918 we reached Fontaine, about five kilometres west of that place. Here we went into the line again for about three weeks. The whole Front was in an unceasing uproar day and night. It blazed *and roared and quivered with incessant explosions. The air was for ever filled with the screaming and the whistling of the shells, the flash and thunder of explosives and their sickly smell. If this wasn't enough, we were on starvation rations now, and suffered agonies from thirst. The baggage waggons and the field kitchens got held up and hopelessly stuck in the wrecked roads to the rear, or came within range of the enemy guns, so that we were cut off even from such supplies as there were. One whole week we got practically nothing. I remember how Hitler and I sometimes, on an extra black night, would crawl out of the trench to scrounge round for something to eat. He'd have an empty petrol can, and I'd have a knife. We hunted round where they'd been slaughtering the horses, and if we could hit on some poor shot beast which didn't stink too badly as yet, we'd slice a bit off his quarter. Hitler'd fill the can with shell-hole water, and, stumbling back again to the dug-out, we'd deliver this booty to the cook! We were a crew of scarecrows, I can tell you, when at last we were relieved, half-starved and with the sore, red eyes of men who haven't had what you could call one decent sleep for nearly a fortnight! We were nothing but a handful of tramps, mud from top to toe, not a whole tunic amongst us. We came out of the line over twelve hundred fewer than we went in.*

They marched us another two or three days to rest billets at Ghery les Poully. For weeks we'd never had our clothes off - now, first to sleep, and then to eat! After that we had a clean-up, if out bits of once-upon-a-time shirts, or remnants of once-upon-a-time boots were yet worth the time and trouble. In the middle of it, though, the alarm was sounded; we were to be rushed to a sector, Anizy-Lizy. Grousing and swearing we limped off again towards the trenches. The Front was roaring and blazing away in full blast. We were only a few hundred strong now, and were sent to hold a line some four miles long, for ten days and nights. We spent hours sheltering in shell-holes, battered with flying clods of earth - when not directly hit by shot and shell - which hit like fists and knocked a man's breath out of his bellows.'

By 26th April 1918 it was obvious that the last great German offensive had already begun to run its course and the 16th RIR, instead of advancing, was now doggedly holding on to defensive positions where it was subject to increasingly heavy artillery barrages. Balthasar Brandmayer later recalled this terrifying period in the history of the 16th RIR:

'After a few days, not one house remained standing in the fire-zones, here and there were piles of rubble, mute testimony to the bloodiest events that had ever taken place on the face of the earth. On bright moonlight nights, the ruins loomed ghostlike over the wide battlefield, reaching heavenwards, as though in mourning for their former splendor.

Dispatch runners lay in the cellar of a badly damaged chateau…. Supplies now so inadequate, that a real famine broke out after eight days. Our group had to make do with a loaf of bread a day between us. Hitler and I often crept out at night and reached the terrain for livestock. Pieces were cut from the cadaver of a horse that was no longer fresh, and with overflowing hearts, handed to our culinary artist. Rain puddles supplied useful water to some extent. And if this made us sick, then it at least suppressed our hunger. The men were becoming jittery. After 26 days, it is high time we were relieved.'

The dejected state of the men of the List Regiment was reflected throughout the army. By May 1918 the Imperial German Army was reaching the very last reserves of its strength. The influx of manpower which had made the great offensive possible had long since been expended and the men were worn down by malnutrition, disease, fatigue and enemy action. The decision to pull the List Regiment out of the line did not come a moment too soon for the wretched survivors who had begun the great push in such high spirits. Ignatz Westenkirchner again takes up the story:

'Then at last, on 15th May 1918, when the 6th Division was relieved, the strength of the List Regiment had dwindled to that of a single company. Many of the chaps had to be carried on stretchers, or helped along somehow, or they couldn't have made the retreat. Two of

us messengers were senseless, and the rest were ghosts rather than men. We filed out of the trenches, as usual, before the greying of the dawn. Muddy and sunken-eyed came the pitiable line of stumbling figures, lots of them with flapping empty sleeves, unbuttoned tunics, and blood-soaked rags bound round head or arm or hand. Others came two by two, leaning on each other, dragging, limping. The stretchers got knocked about over the broken ground. Single figures brought up the rear with rifles and equipment, packs, buckets, and gear of every indescribable description.'

The Imperial German Army was down but not yet out, somehow it still was able to re-group and scrape together sufficient forces for a last series of attacks which initially met with a measure of success. On 30th June 1918 the 16th RIR was ordered to join German forces successfully advancing on the Marne, near Chateau-Thierry. In this last great surge forward the victorious German forces once again tasted a measure of success and advanced 32 miles in just three days, and now came within 50 miles of Paris. The fighting was once more severe and the List Regiment lost 59 men on the first day of fighting, alone. Balthasar Brandmayer again recorded his impressions of the last successful action of the war.

'The enemy is scarcely able to defend himself. Up-hill, down-dale, through thick and thin, we follow on behind his fleeing heels. Trench warfare seems to have been overtaken in full flood by a war of movement. With Hitler, I search for companies that are advancing surprisingly quickly. Searchlights start up and plunge path and wood into an abundance of glaring light. The Froggie had, in between times, reassembled. He desperately resists our assault. We run through a raging fire. Fragments of exploding shells scatter among us. Their flat trajectories drive us to distraction.'

Despite these scattered advances, as 1918 wore on into autumn it was clear that the offensive strategy of 1918 was not working any better than the defensive strategy of 1917. Germany was finished, allied victories outweighed the German advances and the losses were irreplaceable, but despite the signs of impending disaster on the home front and in the field the High Command were intent on trying to attack with the last vestiges of its strength. It was clear that the Imperial German Army was straining every last sinew in the attempt to continue to resist the allied steamroller. There was no time to properly rest and rehabilitate the men who had given so much in the great push. Every unit was required at the front and the men of the List Regiment were soon plunged back into combat.

'It was at this juncture that, according to Ignatz Westenkirchner, Hitler demonstrated his courage and skill as a soldier by capturing a party of French soldiers. Some of Westenkirchner's words undoubtedly ring true, but his description of the episode, complete with Hitler's inner dialogue helpfully set out in detail, does smack of more than a touch of hyperbole: 'On May 26th 1918 our artillery began a fresh attack on the French trenches. Gas followed. The enemy was completely overborne on the Soissons-Fismes sector. We List found ourselves in Juvigny. Then we marched without pause to Epagny. We remained a good long time in trenches between Vezaponin and Nouvron, and spent the first part of June reconnoitring in that region. Then a queer thing happened. It was still day, the 4th June, as a matter of fact, and the firing had died down for the nonce. The sun was hot. Men were sitting about, silent, weary, unsociable, sleepy, reading letters and writing home. Hitler had gone off by himself and must have been half a mile away. He had just surmounted a slight rise in the apparently vacant landscape when suddenly he heard the whirring of a machine-gun and bullets peppered all the air about him. He flung himself face downwards on the ground. The gun ceased fire. Gingerly Hitler essayed to move. Instantly it spat again, lead and fire. At length, however, he managed to worm his way to the next hole, 'Evidently a French ambush,' he thought, 'with a camouflaged gun,' and paused, and thought things over. 'Quite a number of men,' he supposed, and rightly. For within the next ten minutes or so, at least half a dozen of them, fully armed, appeared climbing over the top of the trench. 'One, two, three - five - eight - Donnerwetter!' he thought, 'however many more?' Then like a flash, he leaped to his

feet, dragged his revolver from his belt, and levelling it at the enemy,
shouted at them to surrender. 'Whichever of you budges, he's a dead
man!' Whether the Frenchmen understood what he said or not, they
understood what he meant and promptly fell into line as ordered.
'You're my prisoners! March!' Hitler signalled the way. Off they
went, Hitler in the rear. Perhaps they'd covered a hundred metres this
way, perhaps two, when the whole twelve of them began to wonder
where the rest of the German detail might be which had captured
them. Another hundred metres they plodded silently forward without
a single enemy more showing up than this fellow with the revolver.
'Sacre Nom!' - exclaimed one of them - but got no farther. He found
himself directly menaced by that shining barrel. Forwards! Half a
mile farther and they came to the German trenches, when Hitler
turned the lot over to the company, amid roars of laughter. 'Heavens!
If we'd only known!' muttered the prisoners, 'but the blasted blighter
carried the thing off so mighty high handed!"

If there is even a streak of truth in this account it should come as
no surprise that, in August 1918, Hitler was finally awarded the Iron
Cross First Class. The award of this medal to a member of the rank
and file was highly unusual, this decoration was normally the preserve
of the Officer Corps. There are a number of sceptics in the body of
historians, most notably Thomas Weber, who maintains that Hitler
obtained the award merely because his face fitted in at Regimental
H.Q., but if Westenkirchner is to be given any weight at all then we
must give strong credence to the fact that Hitler certainly did deserve
the award for his conduct in the field. However, despite the unusual
circumstances, Hitler made a typically obdurate decision not to wear the
decoration which was so highly coveted by almost every German soldier.
He perversely continued to sport the ribbon of Iron Cross Second Class
on his tunic and later explained his reasoning during one of his tabletalk
sessions on 15th May 1942:

'During the first World War, I didn't wear my Iron Cross, First
Class, because I saw how it was awarded. We had in my regiment a
Jew named Guttmann, who was the most terrible coward. He had the

Iron Cross, First Class. It was revolting. I didn't decide to wear my
decoration until after I returned from the front, when I saw how the
Reds were behaving to soldiers. Then I wore it in defiance.'

Hitler's bravery had been recognised by his superiors and he was certainly regarded as a first class soldier by his contemporaries. There were ample opportunities for a bold individual such as Hitler to gain such recognition as the 16th RIR was involved in fierce fighting which continued into July 1918 and Ignatz Westenkirchner was able to recall the details for his interview with Heinz A. Heinz:

'After that, the fighting between the Oise and the Marne was
stubborn and bitter beyond description. Step by step we were forced
back by overwhelming numbers. We made a stand along the line
Aisne-Marne, however, from 1st July to the 14th July 1918, from
which the enemy failed to dislodge us. We were relieved on 30th July
1918. They brought us out on the line to go through a ten-day course
of instructions, of which interval we took advantage to get back
somewhat to the semblance of ordinary mortals.'

In the middle of August 1918, the List Regiment once more entrained for the Somme region where they took part in the defence of the sector between Arras and Albert. The men of the 16th RIR and its parent formation, the 6th Bavarian Reserve Division, steadfastly held on to their trenches in a line which ran from Monchy to Bapaume. They doggedly held their ground against a series of savage onslaughts, all of which failed to dislodge the resolute defenders. The Listers remained in the vicinity of Bapaume and fought on there until the end of August 1918 and it was no doubt a great relief when they were ordered to march north east towards the frontier between Belgium and Holland. Not far from Bruges the 16th RIR put in a spell of guardwork on the frontier which included a brief excursion to Ostend.

This welcome visit gave Hitler a respite from the trenches and also the chance to view the Marines who guarded the port. One little known episode took place at this time when Hitler accepted the opportunity to take a tour aboard a U-boat. Over twenty years later on 12th August 1942 during one of Hitler's rambling tabletalks he turned to Admiral

Krancke and recalled the work of Schröder, who had already retired, but who had nonetheless received the order to join up and raise corps of Marines and who rose magnificently to the occasion:

'What we accomplish to-day is child's play in comparison with the efforts we were called upon to make then. Schröder had absolutely nothing! But in no time he was leading his corps to battle. I myself saw these Marines in action for the first time at the Battle of the Somme; and compared with them, we felt we were the rawest of recruits. We then received orders to march to Ostend for a rest. The Regiment arrived there in a most deplorable state. Any Russian regiment, after a five-hundred-mile retreat, would have looked like the Brigade of Guards in comparison. While in Ostend I had the chance of going for a short trip on a submarine, and the sailors, smart, efficient, turned out always as if for a review, were magnificent! It made one ashamed to be seen in their company. I suppose this accounts for the slight inferiority complex which the land forces feel in the presence of the Navy. We had to cut up our great-coats in order to make puttees, and we looked like a bunch of tatterdemalion ballet-dancers! They, on the other hand, looked frightfully smart in their belts and gaiters; and we were not sorry when we escaped to the decent obscurity of our trenches once more.'

The long running saga of the war in the trenches was now rapidly drawing to a close, but for the 16th RIR there was still hard fighting to be done. By September 1918, the brief and merciful respite at Ostend and the Dutch Border was over, and Hitler along with the rest of the Listers found himself in the middle of the last of the fighting which he and Westenkirchner were to see together. For the third time the List Regiment was ordered back to the familiar vicinity of the Ypres salient and, even in the quiet spells, the monotonous bouts of allied shelling continued as grim and unrelenting as ever. By now however, time was running out for Hitler and Westenkirchner later recalled Hitler's last action of the Great War which was played out in the Ypres salient where the whole adventure had begun:

'For the third time we were back on the old ground fought over in 1914. Now we had to defend it, inch by inch, all over again. We *were in the neighbourhood of Gommines; dazed and bewildered with the ceaseless flash and thunder of explosives. Fiercer and fiercer grew the firing. On the night of 13ᵗʰ-14ᵗʰ October 1918 the crashing and howling and roaring of the guns was accompanied by something still more deadly than usual. Our company lay on a little hill near Werwick, a bit to the south of Ypres. All of a sudden the bombardment slackened off and in place of shells came a queer pungent smell. Word flew through the trenches that the English were attacking with chlorine gas. Hitherto the List hadn't experienced this sort of gas, but now we got a thorough dose of it. As I stuck my head outside the dug-out for a quick look round I found myself confronted by a hideous lot of bogies. In the place of men were creatures with visages of sheer horror. At that I shot into my own gas-mask! For hours we lay there with this foul stuff poisoning every gulp of air outside. Suddenly one of the chaps could stand it no longer. He sprang up, wrenched the mask from his head and face, gasping, only to encounter a waft of the white-green poison. It caught him by the throat and flung him back choking, gurgling, suffocating, dying. The gas let off by morning and the shelling began again, to our unbounded relief. Better the deadliest bombardment than that poisoned drowning stifling. How we tore off those masks, and gulped in the air! It was still stinking of the stuff, and reeked again of high explosive, but to us it was the very breath of Heaven. Every now and then the enemy still sent a gas bomb over together with the rest. A man would shriek, throw up his arms, and fling them across his eyes. There was nothing for it but to clap the filthy masks over our heads again. The ferocity of the attack increased. Hour after hour of this inferno went by. It seemed as though that paling in the east which heralded the longed-for dawn would never come again. We chaps just hugged the ravaged and shattered ground, lying, indistinguishable lumps of filth and earth ourselves, within the sheltering lip of the water-filled craters torn up by previous shelling. We were practically finished. Only a handful of us yet remained. Most of us lay there, black bundles, never to move again. As for me, I was at my last gasp. I began vomiting into my own face - wrenched the gas-mask off - and knew no more.*

About seven next morning Hitler was despatched with an order to our rear. Dropping with exhaustion, he staggered off. It was useless by now to count up how many days and nights we'd gone without sleep. His eyes were burning, sore, and smarting - gas - he supposed, or dog weariness. Anyhow, they rapidly got worse. The pain was hideous; presently he could see nothing but a fog. Stumbling, and falling over and over again, he made what feeble progress he could. Every time he went down crash, it was harder and harder to drag himself to his feet again. The last time, all his failing strength was exhausted in freeing himself from the mask... he could struggle up no more... his eyes were searing coals... Hitler collapsed. Goodness only knows how long it was before the stretcher bearers found him. They brought him in, though, at last, and took him to the dressing-station. This was on the morning of October 14th, 1918 - just before the end.'

Even Lucky Linzer couldn't hope to outrun the carnage of the Great War. On 13th October 1918 his store of good fortune had finally run out and, less than a month before the Armistice, Hitler was again admitted to a field hospital. He had been temporarily blinded, not by chlorine gas as Westenkirchner believed, but by a British mustard gas attack. During the night of October 13th-14th, the British had opened an attack with gas on the front south of Ypres using a new strain of the yellow gas whose effect was unknown. Hitler was destined to experience it that very night. On that low hill south of Werwick, in the evening of October 13th, Hitler and his comrades were subjected for several hours to a heavy bombardment with gas bombs, which continued throughout the night with more or less intensity. About midnight a number of Hitler's comrades were put out of action, some forever. Towards morning Hitler also began to feel pain. It increased with every quarter of an hour; and by about seven o'clock his eyes were scorching and he staggered back and delivered the last dispatch he was destined to carry in the Great War. The terrible effect of the gas continued and Hitler vividly recalled its effects:

'A few hours later my eyes were like glowing coals and all was darkness around me. I was sent into hospital at Pasewalk in Pomerania, and there it was that I had to hear of the Revolution.'

In the hospital at Pasewalk Hitler, to his intense relief, was soon beginning to experience signs that he might recover his sight. The burning pain in his eye-sockets had become less severe. Gradually he was able to distinguish the general outlines of his immediate surroundings and the first glimmers of hope arose that he would regain his sight.

Hitler had some reason for optimism in his private world, however the wider picture remained gloomy and the spectre of revolution now loomed over Germany. For some time there had been something in the air which only Hitler failed to recognise as the indefinable hint of insurrection. Although Hitler did not recognise the signs, Germany's strategic situation was becoming unbearable, the tensions were obvious, widespread industrial unrest had led to a munitions strike similar in the spring of 1918, rationing was growing even more strict and something was bound to give within the next few weeks. Rumours were constantly coming from the Navy, which was now in a state of ferment. Hitler later recalled how his fellow patients in the hospital were constantly talking abut the end of the war and hoping that this was not far off. No doubt this would have triggered one of Hitler's trade mark harangues against defeatism especially when faced with three Jewish soldiers who were suffering from veneral disease which was considered a self inflicted wound:

'A few Jew-boys were the leaders in that combat for the 'Liberty, Beauty, and Dignity' of our National Being. Not one of them had seen active service at the front. Through the medium of a hospital for venereal diseases these three Orientals had been sent back home. Now their red rags were being hoisted here.'

Throughout November 1918 the general tension increased. Finally Hitler recalled how one day in November 1918, the outside world suddenly broke in upon the closed world of the hospital. Sailors came in motor-lorries and called on the patients to rise in revolt. Hitler scornfully recalled those startling events as he first thought that this outbreak of high treason was only a local affair. He recalls how he tried to enforce this belief among his wounded comrades. Hitler's Bavarian hospital mates, in particular, were readily responsive. Their inclinations were not revolutionary and Hitler deemed that their loyalty to the Bavarian House of Wittelsbach was stronger than the will of 'a few Jews.' Hitler clung to the belief that this was merely an isolated revolt in the Navy which would suppressed within the next few days.

Hitler was in for a shock. Within the next few days came the most astounding information that was in reality a general revolution. In addition to this, from the front came the shameful news that the army wished to capitulate. On 10th November 1918 the local pastor visited the hospital for the purpose of delivering a short address. It was in this way they came to know the whole shocking story. Kaiser Wilhelm II had abdicated and fled to the Netherlands. A republic had been hastily proclaimed on 8th November 1918, by Social Democrat Philipp Scheidemann in order to prevent a Communist revolution. Hitler was in a fever of excitement as he listened to the address:

'The reverend old gentleman informed the patients that the Prussian House of Hohenzollern would no longer wear the Imperial Crown, that the Fatherland had become a 'Republic'.'

Hitler recalled how a feeling of profound dismay fell on the people in that assembly, and how he broke down completely with the realisation that the war was lost, he said, and Germany was now at the mercy of the victors. Hitler was made painfully aware of the fact that his beloved Fatherland would have to bear heavy burdens in the future. Germany was nonetheless forced to accept the terms of the Armistice and trust to the magnanimity of her former enemies. It was impossible for Hitler to stay and listen to any more of the address. He recalled how darkness surrounded him as he staggered and stumbled back to his ward and buried his aching head between the blankets and pillow. Hitler had not cried since the day that he stood beside his mother's grave but, now, we are told, he wept floods of tears.

'During all those long years of war, when Death claimed many a true friend and comrade from our ranks, to me it would have *appeared sinful to have uttered a word of complaint. Did they not die for Germany? And, finally, almost in the last few days of that titanic struggle, when the waves of poison gas enveloped me and began to penetrate my eyes, the thought of becoming permanently blind unnerved me; but the voice of conscience cried out immediately: Poor miserable fellow, will you start howling when there are thousands of others whose lot is a hundred times worse than yours? And so I accepted my misfortune in silence, realizing that this was the only thing to be done and that personal suffering was nothing when compared with the misfortune of one's country.'*

Heinz A. Heinz writing in 'Germany's Hitler', took up the narrative of Hitler's journey into despair and it provides an interesting glimpse into the histrionic style of Nazi propaganda in the thirties.

'It was in hospital at Pasewalk, in Pomerania, that Adolf Hitler heard of the Revolution, the flight of the Kaiser, and the collapse of the Fatherland.'

His description so closely follows the passage in *'Mein Kampf'* that we must assume Heinz refreshed his memory from Hitler's acccount:

'He had not wept since he stood by his mother's graveside. Now, however, with the gas still "ravening" on his eyes, and threatening him with their total loss, he weeps again. He stumbles away, falls down on his hospital cot, and cries out in anguish all the sacrifice had been in vain! "Would not the graves open of all the hundreds and thousands of those who had left the Fatherland full of high belief and hope, never to return..."'

Hitler now had to face the unpalatable truth that it had all had been in vain. In his anger and despair he instantly formed the view that, what he described as, a gang of despicable criminals, had somehow gotten their hands on the Fatherland. This was to become known as the *Dolchstoss legende*, the belief that the Imperial German Army had been betrayed and had suffered a stab in the back which delivered Germany into the hands of her enemies.

Inevitably Hitler came to lay the blame at the door of the Jews and in a chillingly prophetic passage from *'Mein Kampf'* he outlined what his own solution would have been; it involved the massacre of fifteen thousand Jews by poison gas. It is sobering to realize that within sixteen years from the date on which this passage was written, under the direction of Heinrich Himmler, the actions which Hitler advocated so fervently were being turned into reality on an unimaginable scale:

'At the beginning of the War, or even during the War, if twelve or fifteen thousand of these Jews who were corrupting the nation had been forced to submit to poison-gas, just as hundreds of thousands of our best German workers from every social stratum and from every trade and calling had to face it in the field, then the millions of sacrifices made at the front would not have been in vain. On the contrary: If twelve thousand of these malefactors had been eliminated in proper time probably the lives of a million decent men, who would be of value to Germany in the future, might have been saved.'

It was not just the Jews who bore the brunt of Hitler's pent up wrath. In the pages of *'Mein Kampf'* Hitler reacted with typical psychotic venom to what he imagined was a fully fledged press conspiracy. The more Hitler tried to glean some definite information of the terrible events that had happened, the more his head became aflamed with rage and shame. The following days were terrible for a zealot like Hitler to bear, and during the long nights in Pasewalk his hatred increased for those he perceived to be the orignators of the dastardly crime. Finally, the grand scheme of events became clear to Hitler and he reasoned that Emperor William II was the first German Emperor to offer the hand of friendship to the Marxist leaders, not suspecting, of course, that they were scoundrels without any sense of honour. Hitler envisaged that while they held the Imperial hand in theirs, the other hand was already feeling for the dagger. From that conclusion he moved swiftly on to a new and ominous conclusion. 'There is no such thing as coming to an understanding with the Jews. It must be the hard-and-fast 'Either-Or'.' From that moment onwards it seemed that Hitler decided that he would take up a political career.

Hitler's role in the creation of the Nazi party is well documented and is outside the scope of the present volume, but the story of Ignatz

Westenkirchner is less well known and his life after the Great War makes an interesting epilogue which touches upon the misery endured by many former soldiers during the postwar years of depression and paints a gritty counterpoint to Hitler's glittering rise to fame. His saga was related to Heinz A. Heinz who recorded the story for posterity:

"After that hideous night in Flanders in 1918 when he got gassed," said Westenkirchner, "I never bumped up against Hitler again until we ran across each other here in Munich, in the Sterneckerbrau. That was in the beginning of 1920. I belonged to the Green Police just then - I'd enrolled just after the great bust-up of the Revolution. We old comrades of the List Regiment forgathered at the Sterneckerbrau: Hitler used the place regularly. But in the March of that year I left the police and went home to my own town not far from Munich. Hitler was against it. He did all he could to persuade me to stop where I was. He said he was dead certain he would himself succeed over his own plans and political ideas, and that if I'd only hang on, he would give an eye to me as well. But I wasn't to be turned aside. After a year or two I got into difficulties - couldn't make a go of it - and found myself among the workless and the unemployed. I decided to clear out, family and all, to the U.S.A. At first it wasn't too bad, but things were none too cheerful even over there, and by the beginning of '33 I was as poorly fixed as ever, and out of a job. Anyhow I'd kept up with some of the old List comrades and in the autumn of that year one of them sent me word that Hitler'd like a line from me from time to time. I wrote straightaway to him in Berlin, but got no answer. So I had another shot at it and wrote to his sister at Obersalzberg. And she sent him my news. Not particularly good news - mine! Then, suddenly, one day at Reading in Pennsylvania, where I happened to be living, I got a telegram from a German shipping office informing me that the Führer, Adolf Hitler himself, had defrayed all the expenses of my return with my family to Germany, and that I could set out to come home just as soon as I liked. Overjoyed, the whole lot of us set sail early in December. We reached Hamburg and went on straight to Berlin. I just longed to see my old comrade again - Reichskanzler *though he be - and thank him from the bottom of my grateful heart for having come so splendidly to our rescue.*

I got to the Chancellery and found him just the same as ever. His greeting was as warm as man could wish. He spoke, too, in our local dialect, 'Jolly glad to see you back, Westenkirchner! Suppose you just sit yourself down and tell me all the yarn. We had a good old talk, as you may imagine, and he wound up by saying he'd got a job for me on the party paper here in Munich. Wouldn't hear a word of thanks. I just tried to tell him what I felt and what I thought of him, but laughingly he waived it all aside, 'Take it as read! Take it as read,!' he said, and so I had to.'

- CHAPTER 10 -

THE RETURN TO FLANDERS

IN THE HEADY DAYS OF LATE JUNE 1940 THE jubilant crowds that flocked the streets of Berlin and Munich to celebrate the fall of France hailed Adolf Hitler as a great German hero. They ecstatically proclaimed him the architect of the most stunning victory the world had ever seen and the febrile atmosphere was elevated further by Generaloberst Wilhelm Keitel who dubbed Hitler as 'the greatest general of all time.'

The National Socialist propaganda machine soon added another layer to the triumphalist celebrations, under the masterful control of Doctor Goebbels, the Nazis relentlessly trumpeted the idea that Hitler was a fearless fighter who, for four long years from 1914 to 1918, had served in the face of omnipresent danger. One of Goebbels' key target groups were the millions of new adherents to the Nazi party especially the legions of men who had served in the trenches. They formed the informal *frontgemeinschaft,* or brotherhood of frontline fighters. During the years of turmoil which had followed the Great War many of these men continued under arms and fought on as members of the *Freikorps.* Their support was vital to a party with paramilitary roots and they responded to the idea that Hitler was one of their number who enjoyed their *kameradschaft* - or fellowship.

The Nazi Party had always relied for much of its strength in its appeal to war veterans such as Westenkirchner and made much political capital from the concept of *Frontgemeinschaft.* It was vital therefore that Hitler was accepted by his peers as one who enjoyed acceptance and *kameradschaft.* It was important to him that he should enjoy a reputation as a fearless front-line fighter who had miraculously endured four years of constant danger in the trenches.

Writing in the pages of his semi-autobiographical *'Mein Kampf'*, Hitler contributed his own highly selective account of his war-time service and the legend of the *Fürher* as a bold front-line fighter continued to grow. The Nazi propaganda master plan worked as intended and as a result of Goebbel's efforts millions of Germans, including the former soldiers who formed the *Nationalsocializter Deutscher Frontkämpferbund* (National Socialist League of German Frontline Fighters) unhesitatingly accepted the party line that Hitler had been a valiant hero fighting in the line of fire at the very front-line of the trenches.

By late June 1940 Hitler's political position seemed unassailable, but even in his greatest hour of triumph, the debateable legacy of his service in the Great War loomed over Hitler. He was painfully aware that there were many who doubted his claims and accordingly he lived under the continual shadow of his opponent's allegations that his war record was wildly exaggerated and he was in fact nothing more than an *etapenschweine* (a rear area hog), and worse still, he was reputed to be a cowardly draft-dodger from the Austro-Hungarian army who had spent the First World War safely out of harm's way far behind the lines. Despite all of Goebbel's efforts, throughout the twenties and thirties, there were constant whispers that the myth of Hitler the bold front-line fighter was a lie; a false concoction created by the Nazi spin doctors. For the man who was the figurehead of the *Nationalsocializter Deutscher Frontkämpferbund* this was an embarrassing weakness and it was to become a matter of huge personal importance to Adolf Hitler.

On Sunday 23rd June 1940 Adolf Hitler made his infamous visit to Paris. He was accompanied by his favoured architects Albert Speer and Hermann Giesler. The artistic aspect of the party was completed by the addition of Arno Breker, Hitler's most favoured sculptor. Both Giesler writing in *'Ein Anderer Hitler'* and Breker in his memoirs, state that the trip took place on Sunday 23rd June. However, writing in his book 'Inside The Third Reich', Speer erroneously cites the date as 28th June 1940, but as he describes the moment when the armistice came into effect as part of the trip, the date of the 28th is clearly an error on his part. Giesler later recalled how surprised he was to be stopped by the Viennese police and escorted to Vienna airport where he was placed on a courier aircraft bound for France. However there was a purpose behind Hitler's decision to include the artists. At a personal level Hitler cared nothing for the legendary city and was only interested in Paris for its architecture. The civilian members of his entourage were there to envision how the city could be outdone by the new Berlin visualised by Hitler as the greatest and most imposing city in the world. In order to blend into the background the artist and architects were equipped with military uniforms.

Accompanied by this unusual entourage plus personal photographer Heinrich Hoffman and a news-film crew, Hitler toured the deserted streets of the French capital in the early hours of that infamous Sunday morning. However as the motor cavalcade drove through the lifeless city, with its Gendarmes meekly saluting, even in the moment of his greatest triumph, it seems that there was a lurking pre-occupation in the mind of Adolf Hitler. Paris was the glittering prize for Hitler, and its capture, which had eluded the German generals during the First World War, was a stunning strategic achievement. Hitler confided to Giesler that the capture of the city made him happier than words could express, but Hitler's visit to Paris was remarkably brief. The tour began at 6 A.M., he stopped for perfunctory visits to admire architecture and to visit the Opera House, he visited the Church at Madeleine, Napoleon's tomb and, most famously, stopped at Trocadero to view the environs of the Eiffel Tower where the iconic photograph was taken. By 9 A.M. the tour was over, Hitler would never return to France.

With the brief tour complete, Hitler's aesthetes were verbally charged by him with the job of making the new Berlin grander and more breath-taking than the beautiful French capital. Speer, Breker and Giesler then changed out of their military uniforms and left his entourage. Intriguingly, Hitler's triumphal visit to Paris had lasted only three hours.

No sooner had the artists been despatched to go about their business than they were replaced by two former colleagues from Hitler's old regiment who were to accompany him on the next, and to Hitler, far more important, stage of his journey. Hitler had only hours to spare for his perfunctory Paris visit but, in June 1940, he would find four days to re-visit the Great War battlefields. It was for this purpose that he had summoned two former colleagues to accompany him on a second visit to an insignificant area of Flanders on the border of France and Belgium. Those trusted and hand-picked men were Max Amann and Ernst Schmidt. For Hitler they embodied the idea of the *frontgemeinschaft* and also of *Kameradschaft,* the comradeship which Hitler so desperately sought to be associated with. As part of his entourage Hitler was also careful to once more include Heinrich Hoffman, the man who had captured his first image of Hitler as an insignificant part the Munich crowd in August 1914 and who was now elevated to the role of Hitler's personal photographer. He was there to produce a photographic record of Hitler's triumphant return to the Great War battlefields.

What is highly significant is the fact that this visit was actually the second time during the momentous month of June 1940 that Hitler had found time to come to this militarily unimportant corner where France and Belgium meet. Hitler's first visit to the Great War battlefields of northern France and Flanders actually took place on 1st June 1940. At the time of his visit the battle in France was continuing and the British were still fighting at Dunkirk only 40 miles away. Hitler, as supreme commander, made a routine visit to the Headquarters of von Richenau's 6th Army at Wevelgem, but the staff officers struggling with the logistics of the on-going battle for Dunkirk must have been surprised to be required to suddenly make arrangements for the *Fürher* to drive in a great loop through an area that was still very much a war-zone. The sole purpose of the trip was to allow Hitler to visit some obscure towns and villages which no longer had strategic value in June 1940. The 1st June visit was unexpected and was clearly unnecessary, the circular trip was a frustrating diversion at a time when there were much more pressing calls on Hitler who, as supreme commander, was much in demand elsewhere especially with an undefeated French army still in the field. Amazingly Hitler took with him on his tour Germany's most senior commanders.

By 1st June 1940 it was apparent that the BEF was a beaten force and the withdrawal from the Dunkirk perimeter was already underway, but the British were not beaten yet. At this crucial time, with a strong French army still in the field, General's Wilhelm Keitel and Alfred Jodl were required to join Hitler on what was little more than a glorified trip down memory lane.

The reason for Hitler's diversionary journey was obvious to any German soldier. The itinerary included Menen, Gheluvelt, Ypres, Langemark, Poperinge, Kemel and Wervick. These seemingly unimportant places were actually the sites of the battles of the Great War. This was where the ageing warriors of the *frontgemeinschaft* had served from 1914-18. These towns and villages were the former locations of the front line trenches which had formed the Ypres salient. The RAF and the French Air Force were still operational and during his visit, Hitler's party travelled in armoured Mercedes six wheel staff cars which were guarded by SS men mounting MG34 machine guns. They were also escorted by a mobile Luftwaffe air defence detachment mounting a 2cm flak cannon in case of air attack.

Although he cultivated the impression that he had been ever present in the trenches, Hitler knew the uncomfortable truth behind the myths surrounding his service in the Great War. He knew that, although he held an illustrious war record as a runner, he had not in fact ever been a trench fighter, and in truth had never served a single day in a front-line trench. The plain fact was that, with the exception of the opening battle of his regiment's war at Gheluvelt, Hitler had served for the duration of the Great War as a *meldegänger* in the Headquarters of the 16th Bavarian Reserve Infantry Regiment, and this fact was open to hostile interpretation by anyone with an axe to grind against him.

Hitler has been fiercely criticised and has even been accused, by the highly critical Thomas Weber, of hiding the fact that he was a *meldegänger*. This is certainly not the case, Hitler clearly refers to the fact that when he was gassed in 1918 'I delivered my last despatch.' It is fair to say however that this is the only reference to his actual role in the war.

The simple fact is that Hitler was first and foremost a politician and he was not one to miss a photo-opportunity which was worth its weight in gold in propaganda terms. Here was a golden opportunity to walk down memory lane but at the same time to produce a film and photographic record which would help him to convey the impression that he had constantly been in the thick of things and was a legitimate member of the *frontgemeinschaft* and worthy of his position at the head of the *Nationalsocializter Deutscher Frontkämpferbund*. Despite his unspectacular rank and unglamourous job, for Adolf Hitler, his service in the Great War was a matter of pride which occupied a place of towering significance in his life. By his own account in *'Mein Kampf'*, it defined him as a man. It was against this background that, despite all of the more pressing demands on his time, in June 1940, Hitler twice seized the opportunity to come back to Flanders and recapture the years he treasured. In the process he would, of course, make valuable political capital and shore up the myth that he was entitled to unconditional acceptance and pride of place in the informal ranks of the *frontgemeinschaft*.

On the first of those trips, on 1st June 1940, while the battle for France was still unfolding, Hitler and his entourage took a short flight to the Luftwaffe advance airfield at Evere. From here they mounted a fleet of six wheeled Mercedes and drove in triumph through the deserted streets of Brussels. They then travelled on via Ghent to Ypres where they stopped in Kauwekijnstraat to view the Menin Gate.

The Menin Gate is the imposing monument to the 52,000 British war dead from this sector of the front who have no known grave. To this day the missing British soldiers are commemorated by a moving ceremony which takes place daily. When Hitler came to the town on 1st June 1940 the monument had been damaged by the recent fighting and there was, of course, no question of a ceremony in honour of the men of the British army. Hitler did pause respectfully to study the monument and was no doubt conscious of the fact that some of those men may well have been killed by the Bavarians of Hitler's own Regiment, but the visit to Ypres was brief as the real object of his visit was calling him northwards.

From Ypres, Hitler and his entourage moved on to the German War Cemetery at Langemark which was the main stop on his tour. Today the cemetery is very much the same as it was in 1940, an oasis of sombre and dignified tranquillity. However on the day Hitler made his heavily escorted trip to view the graves of his fallen comrades the Wehrmacht had laid on a guard of honour and as word went round every off-duty soldier in the area swarmed to the site in the hope of grabbing a glimpse of the *Fürher*. The presence of a film crew and Hoffmann's clicking cameras along with the jostling mob of sightseeing *landsers* snapping away on their own cameras robbed the occasion of every shred of sombre dignity, but the publicity goals were achieved and the visit featured heavily in the June edition of *'Deutsche Wochenschau'*. In print the visit was prominently featured in the 13th June edition of the Nazi propaganda magazine *'Illustreiter Beobachter'*. Images from the visit also featured in *'Mit Hitler Im Westin'*, one of the many photo-books published by Hoffman which was a massive best seller in the Third Reich.

Escaping from the crush at Langemark Hitler and his entourage re-boarded their fleet of Mercedes armoured limousines and travelled south via Poperinghe to Kemmel and ascended the local highpoint known as *Kemmelberg* (Kemmel Mountain). Here Hitler enjoyed the panoramic view of the battlefields where his regiment had witnessed tough fighting on numerous occasions between 1914 and 1918. With a detailed map in hand he was able to point out to his entourage the places where he and the List Regiment had seen service.

Next day, on 2nd June 1940, Hitler's entourage came south to Vimy near Arras where the List regiment had fought in 1916 and into 1917. For the genuine members of the *frontgemeinschaft* the collective memory was that the fighting in the German front-line during the battle was relentless and bloody. Their Canadian opponents suffered terribly and today those losses are commemorated by the preserved trenches and memorials. However on 2nd June 1940 it was the German *Fürher* who strutted in triumph through Vimy ridge. Hitler was accompanied throughout his tour by Willhelm Keitel, Germany's most senior Field

Marshal, the irony can't have been lost on Keitel that he was now subordinate to a man who had only ever held the rank of Gefreiter.

On the surface there was very little reason for the enduring controversy which surrounds Hitler's service record. The bald facts of Hitler's military career are very clear and reasonably well documented. At first glance it appears strange that there should be any controversy whatsoever. With such an obvious and apparently flawless military record it is surprising that there should be any room for debate, but Hitler's record has come under attack for a wide variety of reasons.

The controversy was to an extent self-inflicted and had its roots in Munich in 1913 following Hitler's initial failure to attend for service in the Austro-Hungarian army. Regardless of all of the Nazi avowals to the contrary Hitler was never able to shake off that suspicion. He was constantly targeted with the plausible claim that he was in fact nothing more than a cowardly draft-dodger from the Austro-Hungarian army who had spent the First World War out of harm's way far behind the lines. He therefore lived under the continual shadow of his opponents' allegations that he was not actually worthy of acceptance into the ranks of the *frontgemeinschaft* and had no genuine claim to be a part of the mutuality of his former colleagues.

His enemies relentlessly trumpeted the fact that Hitler was not a trench fighter, but actually held a cushy post as a regimental *meldegänger* who saved his own skin by ensuring that he was never promoted beyond the rank of *gefreiter*. In the eyes of his contemporary opponents he certainly was an *etapenschweine* through and through. The case against Nazi portrayal of Hitler as a genuine and relentless front-line trench fighter was pursued by Hitler's opponents throughout the twenties and into the thirties. These rumours appeared freely in the German press and as long as the debate continued over Hitler's claim to be entitled to be counted as one of the front-line band of brothers who formed the *frontgemeinschaft*, the more the legend of Hitler, the rear area malingerer, took root and grew stronger.

In our own world, Thomas Weber is Hitler's harshest critic among serious historians, but by any objective standard, there seems to be no real foundation for many of the criticisms levelled at Hitler as regards his service in the Great War. Weber disregards for example, the award of the Iron Cross First Class, when the evidence points overwhelmingly towards the fact that Hitler was indeed a dutiful and even courageous soldier.

Nonetheless the fact remains by his early actions in Vienna and Munich, Hitler himself played a major role in causing the controversy which perpetuated a century debate. Almost a hundred years later the debate still continues to rage as fiercely as ever; was Hitler a brave and dedicated warrior as his war record suggests, or was he in fact a coward and a malingerer who had run away from his native Austria to avoid conscription and who saw out the war as an *etapenschweine* hiding from danger in the rear areas?

The body of opinion among historians who have written on the subject is firmly divided. Thomas Weber writing in 'Hitler's First War' is harsh and sceptical of Hitler. John F. Williams writing in the unfortunately titled, but otherwise excellent study, 'Corporal Hitler and the Great War 1914-1918', is much more accepting of the facts at face value.

There is no question that the men on the regimental staff had a comparatively easy life they were spared the high mortality which was endured by the men in the trenches. The 16th Bavarian RIR had an establishment of 3000, but over 3700 men were killed serving in its ranks, the vast majority from the front line trenches companies. On the other hand, although there were substantial casualties among the runners in 1914, Hitler and most of his tight-knit group of comrades who served in the Regimental H.Q. of the 16th RIR, and who were pictured together in 1916, actually survived the war.

With such a high level of casualties in the front-line companies and to a lesser extent in the rear echelons there were ample opportunities for promotion, but Hitler was never promoted beyond the rank of *gefrieter*. Throughout the Great War the men serving in the frontline companies of the Imperial German army were under almost intolerable pressure. Constant shell-fire, malnutrition, disease, fatigue, nervous strain, sniper bullets, trench mortars, machine gun fire, plagues of rats, mines and lice were the ever present companions in the trenches. By and large Hitler was able to avoid the worst of these horrors. Comfortably billeted behind the lines in Fournes and elsewhere, Hitler didn't have to face the nightly terror of the possibility of an enemy trench raid or the chilling prospect being sent on a trench raid of his own. Most nights he could sleep in a bed, draw hot rations and enjoy the comradeship of his close knit group of colleagues.

It was this continuing controversy which lurked on in the background during Hitler's first visit to Flanders in June 1940. That initial visit to the battlefields which took place on 1st and 2nd June 1940 may well have been a spontaneous personal pilgrimage, but it also seems to have provoked a new idea in Hitler's mind which precipated the visit on 24th and 25th June 1940. On 4th August 1942, Hitler was to provide a tantalising nugget which suggests he may have been considering facilitating mass tourism by veterans. As usual he was holding forth in one of his interminable monologues and he touched on his visit to Vimy Ridge:

> 'In the present campaign I got my greatest surprise when I revisited Arras. In the old days it was just a mound of earth. And now! Fields filled with blossom and waving corn, while on Vimy Ridge the scars are much as they were, shell-holes and all. I believe it is much the same in the Champagne. The soldier has a boundless affection for the ground on which he has shed his blood. If we could arrange the transport, we should have a million people pouring into France to revisit the scenes of their former struggle.'

France capitulated at midnight on 22nd June 1940, and when he returned to France in triumph on 23rd June 1940, Hitler seems to have been determined to finally lay an old ghost to rest. For Hitler, even 26 years later, the questions over his service in the Great War represented unfinished business, it seems he had a very public point to prove. It was for this reason that Hitler therefore resolved to spend so little time in Paris and so much time in Flanders. He had resolved that he would return to the battlefields of northern France and Flanders and would shamelessly use that second visit to try to cement his reputation as a member of the *Frontgemeinschaft* community of former front line fighters. In the light of this craving for acceptance we can now understand why Hitler brought with him two former colleagues from the 16th Reserve Infantry Regiment who had fought alongside the *Fürher* in the Great War.

On his second visit to Flanders that month, Hitler, Amann and Schmidt visited Rijsel, Fournes, Fromelles, then drove through Armentiers to Ploegstreert, then once more to Mesen and on Witjschaete and Kammel. The party then stopped in Ypres before driving to Dunkirk via Poperinge.

The stop over in Fournes allowed Hitler and his comrades to pose once more in the garden of the house in Fournes where the regimental messengers had once been based. The entourage then moved on to inspect the surviving bunkers here at Fromelles before driving on through Ypres and on to Dunkirk returning through Poperinge, which had remained in British hands during the Great War. The Furher was serenaded by the music of a German military band.

As planned, the carefully photographed and choreographed visit had found its way into the pages of the propaganda press including cinema newsreels such as *'Deutsche Wochenschau'*, the cover of *'Illustreiter Boebachter'* and Hoffman's *'Mit Hitler Im Westin'* but the rumours concerning Hitler's war service were never dispelled, and today, over one hundred years later, we at last know the truth concerning the reason for the return to the battlefields of Private Hitler's war. The second visit was nothing more than a glorified photo opportunity. Hoffman's photographs would provide the proof of Hitler's return to the scenes of his heroic deeds. The visit would then provide propaganda material which would reinforce the partly line which depicted Hitler as the bold front line trench warrior and rightful leader of the *Nationalsocializter Deutscher Frontkämpferbund*, it would also bring him closer to finally achieving acceptance into the ranks of the *frontgemieinschaft*.

Ultimately Hitler was to be disappointed, unconditional acceptance into the *kameradschaft* of front line fighters would never be his to enjoy. In just five years from his triumphal visit to France, he would die a coward's death by his own hand leaving the frontline fighters of the Wehrmacht in 1945 to soldier on in the war he had brought about. The men of 1945 had no option but to face the long march into captivity in Russia where many were forced into slave labour for ten years or more. That was the true nature of comradeship as practised by Adolf Hitler.

Ironically Field Marshall Keitel exhibited the genuine spirit of *kameradschaft*. His sense of honour and duty led him to face the music and that road would lead to Nuremberg where, in 1946, he would to face the hangman's noose.